Compendium of Indian
REAL ESTATE LAWS

Dr. Adv. HARSHUL SAVLA

Ph.D (MU), MMS (JBIMS), LL.M (MU), LL.B (GLC), BMS (NM)

INDIA • SINGAPORE • MALAYSIA

Notion Press Media Pvt Ltd

No. 50, Chettiyar Agaram Main Road,
Vanagaram, Chennai, Tamil Nadu – 600 095

First Published by Notion Press 2021
Copyright © Dr. Adv. Harshul Savla 2021
All Rights Reserved.

ISBN 978-1-63904-512-9

This book has been published with all efforts taken to make the material error-free after the consent of the author. However, the author and the publisher do not assume and hereby disclaim any liability to any party for any loss, damage, or disruption caused by errors or omissions, whether such errors or omissions result from negligence, accident, or any other cause.

While every effort has been made to avoid any mistake or omission, this publication is being sold on the condition and understanding that neither the author nor the publishers or printers would be liable in any manner to any person by reason of any mistake or omission in this publication or for any action taken or omitted to be taken or advice rendered or accepted on the basis of this work. For any defect in printing or binding the publishers will be liable only to replace the defective copy by another copy of this work then available.

TESTIMONIALS

"I have known Dr. Harshul as a through Real Estate Professional who is very well versed about the Sector, I'm sure his experiences will help one and all"

SBI's First Woman Chairperson, Arundhati Bhattacharya

"Congratulations! Dr Harshul for your amazing endeavor of creating one of India's most comprehensive literature on the Real Estate Sector. It is an excellent series of books and great learning for those who have it. I know that you will soon have a much larger audience for your work"

National President NAREDCO, Dr. Niranjan Hiranandani

"This is one of the most comprehensive set of Real Estate Literature, I strongly recommend to all"

President Elect CREDAI National, Boman Irani (Rustomjee)

"Adv. Harshul Savla is a budding and promising Entrepreneur in Real Estate Industry in MMR region with keen insight and grasp of Strategy, Numbers and Statistics. He is a great addition to the Managing Committee Team of CREDAI MCHI"

President CREDAI MCHI, Deepak Goradia (Dosti Realty)

"Harshul is known to me for a decade, he is an astute Advocate and a celebrated Author. His understanding of Real Estate and its nuances is exhaustive. His work will be a reference guide / point for the new entrants in the sector"

President NAREDCO Maharashtra, Ashok Mohanani (Ekta World)

"Real Estate is a very vast subject. There are very few who understand the theoretical and practical nuances of Real Estate Sector, I am glad to note that you have studied the same in great depth and your analysis will be very helpful to the industry."

Chief Engineer (Development Plan) MCGM, Shri V.P. Chithore

"Adv. Harshul Savla has a very good exposure and knowledge of the Real Estate Sector. He has excellent vocabulary skills and speaks with confidence and clarity on matters of Real Estate. I feel his commitment of sharing knowledge inspires many young Real Estate professionals and he is truly focused on bringing a positive impact in the industry in times to come"

President PEATA India, Ar. Samir Hingoo

"Harshul was part of my team, assisting me in executing my responsibilities as a core team member of JLL India. He has a deep understanding of the Real Estate market, trends and policies"

Former CEO & Country Head – JLL India, Ramesh Nair

"Well Researched, I wish this Book all the Success!"

President Bombay Management Association & Director JBIMS, Dr. Kavita Laghate

"Harshul Savla presents a perfect blend of academia and practical hands-on experience. I am proud to see him excel in all fields"

Former Director JBIMS, Dr. Chandrahauns Chavan

"Dr. Harshul is an avid researcher on the subject of Real Estate. I am sure readers will find his work of immense value to them"

Head Department of Law – University of Mumbai, Dr. Rajeshri Varhadi

"Advocate Harshul is a thoughtful researcher and a prolific writer, his ability to make most complex subject; simple and lucid is remarkable. He is extremely insightful on the subject matter of Real Estate. I'm sure he will produce a good read"

CEO Haj Committee of India & Former Registrar University of Mumbai, Dr. M.A. Khan

"I have mentored Harshul's Ph.D. thesis and I am extremely proud of his Research Skills"

Head of Research Department, Sydenham Institute of Management Studies, Dr. R.K. Srivastava

"This book is a must read for all; I personally endorse Dr. Harshul's Research"

CEO Wockhardt Foundation & Executive Director Wockhardt Ltd., Sir Dr. Huzaifa Khorakiwala

"I am sure Dr. Harshul's books will be an ideal start for anyone wanting to understand about Real Estate Sector in India"

COO – P.D. Hinduja Hospital & Medical Research Centre, Joy Chakraborty

"Harshul has a perfect understanding of issues being faced by the Built Environment. He is an excellent Research person, a good mentor for young talent and we are proud to have him on our panel of Guest Faculty at RICS SBE"

Associate Dean & Director – RICS School Built Environment, Amity University Mumbai, Amol Shimpi

"Harshul is one of the young and upcoming participants of today's real estate industry and I'm sure he will go on to shape and influence it in future"

Director Kanakia Group, Ashish Kanakia

"I wish Dr. Harshul's initiative on contributing content around Real Estate in India via this book all the success!"

Director – Asia Pacific Capital Markets, JLL, Priyank Shah

ABOUT THE AUTHOR

Dr. Adv. Harshul Savla (MRICS)

Dr. Adv. Harshul Savla (MRICS) is a Principal Partner of M Realty (Suvidha Lifespaces) which has successfully completed more than 1.2 million sq.ft. in last 30 years across Mumbai City under the able leadership of Mr. Pramesh Rambhiya. CRISIL India recognized Dr. Harshul as "Young Thought Leader" and Realty NXT featured him as "Young Turk of Real Estate Sector". He has won the prestigious CREDAI-MCHI Golden Pillar Award in the category of Best Debutant Real Estate Developer and has been awarded "Young Achiever of the Year" by ET NOW, CNN News 18, ZEE Business, MAHARASHTRA Times, ABP News, MID DAY and Realty Quarter.

About the Author

Dr. Harshul has worked as EA to Ramesh Nair, Former CEO and Country Head at JLL, India and has worked in the Wealth Management Team at TATA Capital where he was awarded the National Award for Exemplary Performance. He is a perfect blend of Corporate Experience along with stellar education credentials of Ph.D., LL.M, LL.B, MBA and BMS.

Dr. Harshul was awarded Doctorate (Ph.D.) for his Thesis on REITs (Real Estate Investment Trusts) which is first such thesis in India on the said subject and the Thesis is also available in the form of a book. Apart from this he is an NSE Certified Market Professional – Level 4 and has done a course on 'Strategic Real Estate Management' from ISB, Hyderabad.

Dr. Harshul is "Co-Chairman: Statistics & Standards" at CREDAI National, which has more than 13,000 Real Estate Developers as its Members and has presence in 217 Cities (21 State Chapters). As a matter of fact, he is one of the youngest Office Bearer in the Managing Committee of CREDAI-MCHI wherein he is the Convener of Research & Analytics Wing and looks into the Learning and Development Initiatives of CREDAI MCHI. Dr. Harshul is also the National Head of the Committee on E-Learning and Masterclass at CREDAI National.

Dr. Harshul is also an Amazon Best Selling Author and has authored one of India's most comprehensive books on Real Estate Sector. Some of his books are: ERA Post RERA, Real Estate Laws, Reality of Realty, Real Estate Valuation, Affordable Housing, NBFC & HFC Crisis, Fractional Ownership & REITs, Insolvency & Bankruptcy Code, Self-Redevelopment & Reviving Stalled Projects, Luxury Retail and COVID-O-NOMICS. He regularly writes articles for fortnightly business magazine "Property House".

About the Author

Dr. Harshul is also a Visiting Faculty at the prestigious RICS School of Built Environment, Mumbai Campus. He teaches the subject 'Real Estate Development Process' to Management Students at the Mumbai Campus. He is also Guest Lecturer at REMI – The Real Estate Management Institute, Mumbai. He was Invited to conduct Session on REITs in India for Developers Members of NAREDCO and was one of the youngest Member Developer to do so. He has also delivered a lecture at PEATA (I) on Future of Realty.

RESEARCH TEAM

Aashish Ahuja

MBA – Law (SBM, NMIMS)

LL.B (University Institute of Legal Studies, H.P. University)

Abhinav Mahajan

MBA – Law (SBM, NMIMS)

LL.B (Guru Gobind Singh Indraprastha University, Delhi)

Adarsh Kanakal

MBA – Law (SBM, NMIMS)

LL.B (Mumbai University)

Arjun Kumar

MBA – Law (SBM, NMIMS)

LL.B (Amity University, Noida)

Bhavesh Patil

PGDM – REM (SBM, NMIMS)

BE – Civil Engineering (Mumbai University)

Roopam Mishra

MBA – Law (SBM, NMIMS)

LL.B (School of Law, KIIT, Bhubaneswar)

Shanya Agarwal

MBA – Law (SBM, NMIMS)

LL.B (Mody University, Sikar, Rajasthan)

Snigdha Ravuri

MBA – Law (SBM, NMIMS)

LL.B (ICFAI Law school, Hyderabad)

CONTENTS

1. Indian Contract Act — 15
2. RERA — 27
3. Consumer Protection Act — 41
4. Securitisation And Reconstruction of Financial Assets And Enforcement of Security Interest (SARFAESI) Act — 48
5. FEMA — 59
6. MRTP Act — 77
7. Land Acquisition Rehabilitation and Resettlement Act, 2013 — 88
8. Benami Property & Enemy Property — 97
9. The Competition Act, 2002 — 107
10. The Transfer Of Property Act, 1882 — 117
11. Insolvency and Bankruptcy Code — 136
12. GST and Capital Gains — 150
13. Registration and Stamp Act — 163
14. Model Tenancy Laws — 175
15. Maharashtra Co-Operative Societies Act — 184
16. Easement Act — 206

17. Development Control and Promotions Regulation 2034   249
18. Slum Rehabilitation Authority   273
19. Ease Of Doing Business and Single Window Clearance   283
20. Environmental Laws   291

CHAPTER 1

INDIAN CONTRACT ACT

The Indian Contract Act is one of our country's oldest commercial statutes. It went into effect on September 1, 1872, and it applies to all of India except Jammu and Kashmir. It is the primary law governing contracts in India, with a total of 266 parts. Let us have a look at some of the most critical aspects of it.

Q1. What is a Contract under the Indian Contract Act,1872?

Ans: The Indian Contract Act, 1872 defines the term "Contract" under its section 2 (h) as "An agreement enforceable by law". To put it another way, a contract is a legal arrangement and enforceable by the country's law.

There are two main elements in this definition: "agreement" and "enforceable by statute."

To put it another way, an agreement is a promise that has been agreed upon by all parties interested in or influenced by it. As a result, this concept incorporates a flow chart or a series of steps that must be followed to construct or draught a contract. The steps can be summarised as follows:

The definition requires a person to whom a certain proposal is made.

The person (parties) in step one has to understand all the aspects of a proposal fully.

"signifies his assent thereto" – means that the person in point one accepts or agrees with the proposal after having fully understood it.

Once the "person" accepts the proposal, the status of the proposed changes to "accepted proposal".

"accepted proposal" becomes a promise. Note that the proposal is not a promise. For the proposal to become a promise, it has to be accepted first.

In other words, when a proposal is made by one or more of the participants who are affected by the proposal, it is approved by all of the parties to the agreement. To summarise, the following information can be interpreted in the following way:

Agreement = Offer + Acceptance.

CONTRACT - According to sec.2(h), a contract is defined as an agreement enforceable before the law.

AGREEMENT - According to sec.2(e), every promise or set of promises forming consideration for each other.

PROMISE - According to sec.2(b), when a person made a proposal to another to whom proposal is made, if proposal is assented there to.

As a result, for an agreement to become a contract under the Act, it must give rise to or contribute to legal obligations, or in other words, it must fall within the legal framework. As a result, we can sum it up as Contract = Accepted Proposal (Agreement) + Legally Enforceable (defined within the law).

Q2. What are the Essentials of a Valid Contract?

Ans: The Essentials of a Contract are specified and listed in the Indian Contract Act, 1872, either directly or by an interpretation by the Indian judiciary in various judgments. Section 10 of the contract enumerates those points that are required for legitimate contracts, such as free consent, the parties' competence, and legal consideration.

- Two parties

    For a contract to be valid, it must include at least two parties. One of these parties will propose, and the other will finally approve it. Both parties must be natural persons or have what is regarded as a legal existence, such as corporations, colleges, associations, and so on.

    For Example: In the case of the State of Gujarat vs Ramanlal S & Co. – A business partnership was dissolved and assets were distributed among the partners as per the settlement. However, all transactions that fall under a contract are liable for taxation by the office of the State Sales Tax Officer. However, the court held that this transaction was not a sale because the parties involved were business partners and joint owners. We need a buyer (party one) and a seller (party two) for sale, which must be different people.

- The intent of Legal Obligation

    The parties to a contract must have firm intentions of entering into a legal agreement with one another. This means that agreements that are not legally enforceable, such as social or domestic agreements between families or neighbours, are not enforceable in a court of law and cannot constitute a binding contract.

- Possibility Of Performance Of an Agreement

    Assume two parties reach an agreement in which person A agrees to bring back the life of person B's deceased relative. Even if both parties agree and all other contract conditions are met, this is not true since resurrecting anyone from the dead is an impossible job. As a result, the agreement cannot be executed, and the contract is invalid.

- Free Consent of the Parties

    Consent is required for an agreement to be formed and thus necessary for a legal contract. Two people are said to commit to the promise if they enter a similar agreement in the same sense. However, for a contract to be binding, we must have free consent, which means that neither party was influenced, forced, misrepresented, or deceived into consenting. In other words, if either party's consent is intentionally or unknowingly revoked, the contract between the parties is rendered null and void.

- Competency of Parties

    Section 11 of the Indian Contract Act, 1872 is:

    "Who are competent to contract — Every person is competent to contract who is (1) of the age of majority according to the law to which he is subject, and who is (2) of sound mind and is (3) not disqualified from contracting by any law to which he is subject."

Let us see these qualifications in detail:

- Refers to the fact that the person must be at least 18 years old or more.

- This means that the party or the person should be able to fully understand the terms or promises of the contract at the time of the formulation of the contract.

- States that any other legal ramifications should not disqualify the party. For example, if the person is a convict or an alien enemy, they may not enter into a contract.

- Lawful Consideration

- In Section 23 of the Act, the unlawful considerations are defined as all those which:

- It is forbidden by law.

- It is of such a nature that, if permitted, it would defeat the provisions of any law or is fraudulent.

- Involves or implies injury to the person or property of another.

- The Court regards it as immoral or opposed to public policy.

These conditions will render the agreement illegal.

Q3. What do you understand by the term 'Consideration'?

The expression 'consideration' in general means the price paid for an obligation. According to Section 2 (d) of the Indian Contract Act, 1872 when at the desire of the promisor, the promisee or any other person has done or abstained from doing, or does or abstains from doing or promises to do or abstain from doing something, such an act or abstinence or promise is called a consideration for the promise. Thus, on analysing the above definition, the following ingredients are essential in understanding the meaning of the term consideration:-

1. Consideration to be given at the desire of the promisor.
2. Consideration to be given by the promise or any other person.

3. Consideration may be past, present or future, in so far as the definition says the promise has done

   i. An act, i.e. doing something

   ii. An abstinence or forbearance, i.e. abstaining or refraining from doing something, and

   iii. A return promise. The general rule is that an agreement made without consideration is void.

4. There must be an act, abstinence or promise by the promisee, which constitutes consideration for the promise

Q4. What is the relevance of a Contingent Contract in Real Estate?

Ans: A Contingent Contract is a contract wherein one party to the contract performs his duties when the other party meets certain conditions. It is dependent upon the happening of a particular event. In a Real Estate Contract, a contingency is a provision that makes the contract null and void if a party to the contract does not perform certain events.

Illustration- A is a builder of an Apartment and B is the Buyer of a Flat. B tells A that if A will complete the flooring of the flat, then B will pay the amount which stands due on his part. This is a situation wherein the Provision of Contingency comes into the picture.

Q5. How is Enforcement of Contingent Contract done in Real Estate?

Ans: As we all know about a Contingent Contract it is necessary to know about the Enforcement of such contracts as per the land law. According to section 32 of the Contract Act, 1872, a contingent contract is a contract to do anything if a future occurrence occurs, and it can be enforced by law if those events occur, or it can be null and void if the events do not occur, and it cannot be enforced by law.

Illustration- A is a builder of an Apartment and B is the Buyer of a Flat. B tells A that if A will complete the flooring of the flat, then B will pay the amount which stands due on his part. If the builder does the flooring, it will be enforced by law as the provision of Contingency has been met by the builder and if it does not complete the flooring, it will not be enforced by law will stand null and void.

Q6. Discuss the contract that becomes void on specified events within a fixed time in Real- Estate?

Ans: A Contingent contract may become void on the happening of such specified events within a fixed time if such event as mentioned becomes impossible, or such event is completed after expiration of the fixed time or such event as mentioned is not completed.

Illustration- A buyer of a flat wants certain amenities of the flat to be changed. The developer does not make any change to the apartment and hand it over to the buyer. Here the contingent contract becomes void as such specified event does not occur in due course of the time.

Q7. Discuss how the contingent Agreement becomes void?

Ans: As per Section 36 of the Indian Contract Act, 1872, The Contingent Contract becomes void if the event specified by one party becomes impossible and such event is not known to be impossible while the parties were entering into an agreement/contract.

Here two stakeholders are in question

Buyer- In a contingent contract, there are two parties to such a contract and one of them is the buyer. So the buyer provides a certain specified event that needs to be completed by the developer, or else the contingent contract will become null and void.

Developer- In a Contingent Contract, the Developer needs to make the changes as mentioned by the Buyer so that the Contingent contract can be enforced under the law of the land.

In the Case of Gian Chand vs Gopala, The contract in question is a contingent contract based on uncertain future events (here is a case of suppression of tact even otherwise) that event having occurred by notification issued under s.6, the contract became impossible of performance. Therefore, it got frustrated and the contracting party is entitled to enforce the terms of the contract for a refund of earnest money. The Trial Court had rightly decreed the suit for return of the earnest money.

Q8. Discuss the obligation of the parties to the contract on the performance of the contract?

Ans: The parties to a contract must keep their respective commitments made when they sign the contract. A promise, therefore, obligates the contracting parties to fulfil their obligations. The general rule of excellence is that the duty must be fulfilled in its entirety on both ends.

There is an exception to the performance of the contract, which is the "De-Minimis" rule.

Q9. Discuss how a contract must be performed in Real Estate Sector?

Ans: In Real Estate, the Developers are generally the promisor to the contract who performs the duties promised by them to the Buyer. In such cases, the promisor himself performs the duties mentioned in section 40 of the Indian Contract Act, 1872. The Developer can come up with a joint agreement with a contractor to perform his duty. And if the Buyer in the contract feels that the duties are not being performed, the buyer can compel anyone from the joint Agreement to perform the duty as prescribed when the buyer had entered the contract to purchase the flat from the developer.

Q10. Discuss the time and place for the performance of the contract in the Real-Estate sector?

Ans: To understand the time and place for the performance of the contract in the Real-Estate Sector, we can understand the same through an excellent case of Hind Construction Contractors v. the State of Maharashtra (1979) the Appellant entered into a contract with the respondent on July 2, 1955, for some construction work with the condition that the contract should be completed within 12 months from the commencement of the work. The Appellant could not complete the work within the stipulated time and the Respondent cancelled the contract with effect from August 16, 1956. The Appellant contended that time was not of the essence and further because of several difficulties, such as excessive rains, lack of proper road and means of approach to the site, and delayed completion.

Q11. Under what circumstances the contract need not be performed in Real-Estate Sector?

Ans: The situation when in a contract the work specified becomes impossible results in a void contract, as mentioned in section 56 of the Indian Contract Act, 1872. Alternatively, when the parties to a contract make some changes or alterations to the clauses in the contract and develop a new contract, the previous contract becomes void, as mentioned in section 62 of the Indian Contract Act,1872.

Illustration- Previously, the buyer and the developer had entered into a contract when the buyer decided to purchase the flat. If there are certain changes to the clauses in the contract with the consent of both the developer and the buyer, then the previous contract stands void and the new contract with the changes made as per the needs will be performed further.

Q12. Discuss the Consequences of Breach of Contract in Real Estate Sector?

Ans: The contract contains certain terms and conditions that play an integral role in the contract's performance. A breach of contract happens when one of the contract's parties fails to perform any of the contract terms. Sections 73-75 of the Indian Contract Act of 1872 address the repercussions of contract violation. Real Estate Contracts include residential and commercial building property and land usage and boundary agreement breach. As per section 75 of the act, A person is entitled to compensation for the damage caused to him which he has sustained through non-fulfilment of the contract if he rightfully rescinds a contract.

Illustration- A buyer has selected a property for which he enters into a contract with the developer to purchase the flat. If there is any sort of non -performance from both parties, then it will be a breach of the contract for non-performance of the contract. There is a remedy for the buyer if the developer makes a non-performance and vice versa.

Q13. Discuss the breach of contract wherein the penalty is stipulated?

Ans: As per section 74 of the Indian Contract Act, 1872, when the parties to the contract have made a clause wherein if there is a breach of contract and a fixed amount of penalty is stipulated, then in such cases, if there is a breach of contract the party who has broken the terms and conditions of the contract needs to pay the fixed sum of money to the party who suffered damages without getting into how much damage he has suffered.

Illustration- A buyer has selected a property for which he enters into a contract with the developer to purchase the flat. If there is any sort of non-performance from both parties, it will be a breach of the contract for the non-performance of the contract and if the contract has the clause wherein the penalty amount is fixed, then only the fixed amount will be received for the damage caused.

Q14. Discuss the Agent and Principal Relationship in a Real Estate Contract?

Ans: In Real–Estate, the Developer can agree with a contractor to construct a building. Here in such cases, the contractor can work as an agent for the Developer. The Developer in such cases can be termed as Principal and the Contractor can be known as the Agent. The Contractor (Agent) can have both express and implied authority while doing the work.

Q15. Discuss the Termination of Agent and Principal relationship in a Real-Estate Contract?

Ans: As per section 201 of the Contract Act, A Developer (Principal) can terminate the agent from working if the construction is fully complete, or the agent (contactor in real estate cases) refuses to work for the principal, or if the Developer revokes his authority for termination of such relationship.

Q16. Can a Contractor have a lien over the developer's property?

Ans: Yes, as per section 221 of the Contract Act, if the contractor and the developer have the relationship of the Agent and Principal, then the agent can retain the principal's goods until he has been settled with all the dues and disbursements which the agent is entitled to.

A purchasing agent can exercise a lien over the goods purchased for his principal until the amount due to him for such purchases has been paid. Such right is, however, subject to an agreement to the contrary. Moreover, such a right is lost when the agent parts with the possession of the goods. The position in this regard was thus explained by Hegde, J. in Ram Prasad V. State of M.P.:

Illustration- A Contractor has been assigned with certain work and the developer has promised to pay the dues after the work is fully completed. If the Developer does not settle the dues of the contractor, then the contractor can retain the developer's property if they have an Agent and principal relationship.

Q17. Discuss the duty of an agent in performing the duties?

Ans: When the contractor and developer come together for an Agent Principal relationship, the agent must perform his duties as per the principal's directions and in good faith and be responsible for the profit earned/losses suffered. The agent must perform the job assigned to him diligently and with due care as if he is working on his project. The Agent is also accountable to the principal when needed.

Illustration- When the developer provides a certain direction in which the contractor needs to work, the contractor needs to follow the direction and work in good faith.

CHAPTER 2

RERA

To facilitate transparency in the home buying process, the Indian Government passed the RERA Act in May 2016. Soon after, RERA was brought into action to address homebuyers, builders, brokers, and other real estate industry stakeholders. Since its inception, RERA has implemented many reforms and more are on the anvil. That is why, as a home buyer or a builder, knowing RERA rules and guidelines will help you navigate the real estate landscape with ease.

So please take a closer look at RERA, its impact, and more.

Q1. Discuss the Real Estate projects registration and its importance?

Ans: As per the recent amendments and changes in the law, a developer can market the project after getting a registration from the Regulatory Authority. If any ventures have already begun, the developer must obtain registration within three months of the act's enactment.

Q2. Discuss the exemption granted for the registration of the project under the act?

Ans: The act provides certain exemptions wherein the developer need not undergo a registration under the regulatory authority for the project. If the project does not exceed 500 square metres or the number of apartments does not exceed eight inclusive of all the phases, for search project registration is not required, or If the completion certificate has already been received for the project by the promoter before the commencement of the Act, then registration is not required for the said project or Registration is also not required for any renovation redevelopment of the building.

Q3. Discuss whether the regulatory authority can revoke the registration for a project?

Ans: Yes, the registration of the project can be revoked by the authority if:

a. the promoter has done any default under the Act or the rules, or

b. the promoter has indulged in any kind of unfair trade practices, or

c. the promoter violates any conditions stated while approving by the Authority.

There is a catch over here: the registration granted shall not be revoked if the promoter has not been given 30 days written notice.

Q4. Discuss the consequences of revocation of such registration of the project?

Ans: Yes, there are certain consequences of revocation of the registration of the projects. Some consequences are as follows:

a. The authority debars the promoter from allowing access to his project's website and other authorities will be informed about the revocation of such registration.

b. The Authority shall freeze the bank accounts of the said project.

c. The Authority shall protect the interest of allottees.

d. The promoter's name will be listed in the name of defaulters and his photograph will be displayed on the website.

e. Under section 8 of the RERA Act, 2016 the remaining development work is to be carried out, which includes consequent de-freezing of the account to facilitate remaining development works.

Stakeholders that are in question are

1. Regulatory Authority- The authority has the supreme power to provide the registration for a specified project. If the Authority feels that the developer is cheating somehow, it may revoke the registration granted to the developer. It needs to keep an eye on all the real estate developers to protect the allottees and provide certain rules as it deems fit, which will protect the public's interest at large.

2. Developer/Promoter- A promoter/ developer needs to take the registration for projects in which he wants to advertise or invite people to invest. Registration is mandatory so that it helps the public to know about the developer and be assured that the investment they are making will not go in vain.

Q5. Describe the functions of a promoter in a real estate business?

Ans: Some of the Functions of the Developer/Promoter in a Real-Estate Business are as follows:

a. He has to provide the details of the registration granted by the authority;

b. He has to update the number of apartments booked every quarterly;

c. He has to update the list of approvals taken and the pending approvals which need to be taken in mere future;

d. He has to update the status of the project;

e. He shall provide the details of the project along with the registration number in the prospectus;

f. All the outgoings need to be paid until he transfers the physical possession of the real estate project to the allottee;

g. The promoter must adhere to the plan approved by the authority;

h. Consent must be taken to transfer the real estate project to a third party from 2/3rd of the allottees and the concerned authority.

Certain responsibilities of the Promoter are as follows-

a. The Promoter is liable for all commitments, functions, and functions under the arrangements of this Act or the standard;

b. The Promoter is responsible for obtaining the completion certificate;

c. The real estate project is developed on leasehold land; the Promoter is responsible for obtaining the lease certificate.

d. The Promoter is responsible for maintaining and providing the essential services;

e. The promoter should enable the formation of an association;

f. All such other details as may be specified should be prepared and maintained by the promoter.

Q6. Can a promoter accept the advance or deposit for blocking the apartment?

Ans: Yes, if the promoter has entered into a written agreement for sale with the buyer and has registered the agreement for sale, he can accept the advance or deposit for blocking the apartment. A promoter can only accept 10% of the total cost of an apartment as a down payment.

Q7. What are the developer's obligations towards a person who suffered losses for any false statement provided in the advertisement?

Ans: The Developer will pay compensation to the person who suffered damages due to the false information provided in the advertisement basing on which he made the advance payment for blocking the apartment.

Illustration- A person who purchased an apartment on having a look at the prospectus and the advertisement published by the developer suffered damages as there was false information in the advertisement. Hence the developer needs to pay the compensation for damages suffered by him.

Q8. Describe the Rights and Duties of the Allottee in a Real Estate Contract?

Ans: The rights and duties of the Allottee in a Real Estate contract are as follows:

a. Allottee is entitled to obtain the information relating to the apartment which the Authority approves;

b. The allottee has the right to know the project's stage-by-stage completion schedule.

c. Allottee is entitled to claim the possession of the apartment;

d. Allottee is entitled to claim the refund of the amount paid along with interest at such rate as may be prescribed;

e. Allottee is entitled to have the necessary documents and plans of the apartment;

f. For any delay in payment, the allottee is entitled to pay the interest at such a rate as may be prescribed.

The Stakeholders that are in question are –

1. Promoter- There are certain duties that a promoter needs to follow to save his registration. If the promoter does not follow such duties as prescribed, his registration might get cancelled and he might be debarred from further registrations from the concerned authority.

2. Allottee- The Allottee has certain duties he must follow when he enters into an agreement with the developer.

Q9. Discuss the functions of the Central Advisory Council.

Ans: There are certain functions of the council so that the policies are formed with consultation with the central government to ensure full growth and development in the Real Estate Sector.

Q10. Discuss the Appellate Tribunal under the Act.

Ans: The Appellate Tribunal is formed to provide justice to the promoters as well as the allottees who suffered damages. As specified in the Act, the Appropriate State Government shall establish an Appellate Tribunal.

Q11. Discuss the power of the Tribunal under the Act.

Ans: The principles of natural justice shall guide the Tribunal established by the Act. The Tribunal under the act shall have the same power as other courts do have under the Code of Civil Procedure. The Tribunal under the Act has the power to regulate its procedures.

Q12. Discuss the Orders passed by the Hon'ble Tribunal.

Ans: The orders passed by the Hon'ble Tribunal are executable as a decree of the civil court. The Tribunal under the act may transmit any order passed by it to a court having local jurisdiction and such court shall execute the decree.

Q13. Discuss the Appeal made to the High Court.

Ans: Any party who is aggrieved by the order passed by the Hon'ble Tribunal can appeal to the High Court within 60 days of the order passed by the Tribunal.

Q14. How does RERA benefit Buyers?

Ans: There are a few ways in which buyers are likely to benefit from the RERA Act:

1. Builders will be unable to postpone projects – Under RERA, not obtaining possession of apartments from the builder will no longer be an issue.

2. Builders will no longer be able to charge for the excess area- Previously, builders could charge for built-up and super built-up areas. Before changing the design or any other structure of a project, developers will also need the approval of two-thirds of the buyers.

3. Builders will be held liable for any defects in construction- Many buyers have expressed concern about the quality of construction. The developer under RERA must repair any structural defect that occurs to the property for up to five years from the date of handing over possession.

4. Builders will not be able to use your money for another project-Delivery of real estate projects on time has been the biggest stumbling block for buyers. However, under RERA, the developer must deposit 70% of the money received from buyers into an escrow account.

5. Grievances will be addressed and resolved quickly- Under RERA, each state will establish regulatory bodies and appellate tribunals to resolve builder-buyer disputes. Any person who

is dissatisfied with a direction can expect a resolution from the appellate within 120 days.

6. Builders will need all clearances before selling – Previously, builders frequently sold projects that did not have all clearances, causing numerous issues for buyers. Under RERA, builders and agents will be required to register with the regulator, disclose all project details, and only sell projects once all necessary clearances have been obtained.

All builders and agents must register with the Regulatory Authority after its establishment.

Q15. What are the Major Benefits of the RERA Act for Buyers?

Ans: The five major benefits of the RERA Act for home buyers are as follows:

a. Right to Information About the Property- This is one main advantage of the RERA act favouring the home buyer. This information can help you on multiple fronts. The developer is entitled to share all the details regarding the project such as plan layout, plan of execution, completion stages, the status of the competition, etc.

b. Standardised Carpet Area – RERA defines carpet area as 'the net usable floor area of an apartment, excluding the area covered by the external walls, areas under services shafts, exclusive balcony or verandah area and exclusive open terrace area, but includes the area covered by the internal partition walls of the apartment'.

c. Builders Will Be Held Responsible for Any Defect/Fault in The Construction- Under the RERA act, if there is any defect or fault in the construction of your apartment, the repairing must be done by the real estate developer. This is for the structural defect in the property for up to 5 years from the date of possession. The repairing has to be done within 30 days once the fault is detected.

d. Grievances Will Be Addressed and Solved Quickly.

e. Builders Will does not Be Able to Delay Projects-According to the RERA act, and each real estate developer must provide a delivery date for the handover of apartment possession. If the builder is unable to complete the project by the delivery date, they will face penalties.

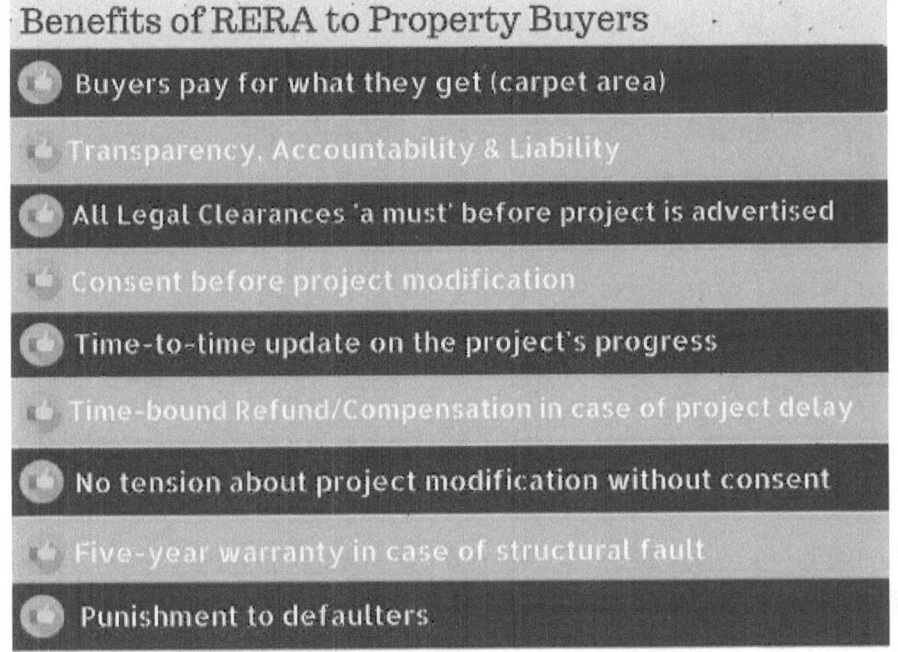

Q16. Can the developer treat covid-19 as 'Force Majeure' under RERA?

Ans: As per the recent announcement made by the Hon'ble Minister of Finance stated that Ministry of Housing and Urban Affairs would issue an advisory to states and urban territories and their regulatory authorities to extend the registration and completion date by six months for all registered projects expiring on or after March 25, 2020, without individual applications.

Adverse impact due to Covid-19 and projects stand the risk of defaulting on RERA timelines. Timelines need to be extended. The housing ministry will also advise states/union territories and their regulatory authorities to the following effect:

- Treat Covid-19 as an event of "Force Majeure" under RERA.
- Regulatory authorities may extend this for another period of up to three months if needed
- Issue fresh "project Registration Certificates" automatically with revised timelines
- Extend timelines for various statuary compliances under RERA concurrently

These measures will de-stress real estate developers and ensure the completion of projects so that the home buyers can get delivery of their booked houses with new timelines as mentioned by the Hon'ble Minister.

Q17. A Recent Judgement of Halliburton Offshore Services v. Vedanta Ltd?

Ans: The grounds taken to invoke the Force Majeure clause are that due to the outbreak of COVID-19, experts from France who may be required cannot travel to India. Since the Force Majeure clause in the contract covers epidemics and pandemics, the Contractor claims that its non-performance is justified and the invocation of Bank Guarantees is liable to have stayed. There is no doubt that COVID-19 is a Force Majeure event.

The past non-performance of the Contractor cannot be condoned due to the COVID-19 lockdown in March 2020 in India. The

Contractor was in breach since September 2019. Opportunities were given to the Contractor to cure the same repeatedly. Despite the same, the Contractor could not complete the Project. The outbreak of a pandemic cannot be used as an excuse for the non-performance of a contract for which the deadlines were much before the outbreak itself.

The question as to whether COVID-19 would justify non-performance or breach of a contract has to be examined on the facts and circumstances of each case. Every breach or non-performance cannot be justified or excused merely on the invocation of COVID-19 as a Force Majeure condition. The Court would have to assess the conduct of the parties before the outbreak, the deadlines that were imposed in the contract, the steps that were to be taken, the various compliances that were required to be made and only then assess as to whether, genuinely, a party was prevented or can justify its non-performance due to the epidemic/pandemic. The settled position in law that a Force Majeure clause is to be interpreted narrowly and not broadly. Parties should be compelled to adhere to contractual terms and conditions, and excusing non-performance would only be in exceptional situations.

It is also not the duty of Courts to provide a shelter for justifying non-performance. There has to be a 'real reason' and a 'real justification' which the Court would consider to invoke a Force Majeure clause.

Q18. Discuss the Punishment for non-registration under the Act?

Ans: If the developer violates the provisions of Section 3, he will face a penalty of up to 10% of the estimated cost of the real estate project as determined by the Authority. If the developer fails to comply with the orders, decisions, or directions issued under section 3, he shall be punished by imprisonment for a term of up to one year.

Q19. What are the penalties and punishment granted by the Hon'ble court if the Developer provides any false information while registering the project under the Regulatory Authority?

Ans: If the developer provides false information or violates the provisions of Section 4, he will face a penalty of up to 5% of the estimated cost of the real estate project, as determined by the Authority.

Q20. What are the penalties and punishment granted by the Hon'ble court if the Developer contravenes any other Act provision?

Ans: If the promoter contravenes any other provisions of this Act, the developer shall be liable to a penalty which may extend up to five per cent of the estimated cost of the real estate project as determined by the Authority.

Q21. What are the penalties and punishment granted by the Hon'ble court if the Developer fails to comply with the orders of the Regulatory Authority?

Ans: If the developer fails to comply with the Regulatory Authority's orders, he will be subject to a penalty of 5% of the estimated cost of the real estate project as determined by the Authority for each day that the default continues.

Q22. What are the penalties and punishment granted by the Hon'ble court if the Developer fails to comply with the orders of the appellate tribunal?

Ans: If the developer fails to comply with the orders of the appellate tribunal than, he shall be punishable with imprisonment for a term which may extend up to three years or with a fine for every day during which such default continues, which may cumulatively extend up to ten per cent of the estimated cost of the real estate project.

Q23. Discuss the Compounding of the offences under the Act?

Ans: If the developer is sentenced to imprisonment under this Act, the court may compound the sentence on such terms and conditions either before or after the prosecution is instituted.

Q24. What are the factors that are to be taken into account by the Adjudicating Officer?

Ans: While adjudging the quantum of compensation or interest, the adjudicating officer shall have due regard to the following factors, namely:

a. the amount of disproportionate gain or unfair advantage, wherever quantifiable, made as a result of the default;

b. the amount of loss caused as a result of the default;

c. the repetitive nature of the default;

d. such other factors which the adjudicating officer considers necessary to the case in furtherance of justice

Developers are those people who make the full utilisation of the land by making good properties in it. The most amazing feature of such legislation is that the developer now needs to keep around 70% of the money received from the customers in a separate account. This will be used proportionally with the construction completed and will undergo audit from time to time. Now the developer cannot make any changes to the approved plan without taking the consent of the allottees. The new law has been stringent for the developers as they need to pay compensation in case of any delay from their side. Previously the promoter used to divert the funds of one project to another. The promoter cannot divert the fund of one project to another after the onset of the new law, i.e. RERA. The promoter can acquire a piece of land only through the land development agreements with the landowners. For the smooth running of their business, the government authorities need to streamline the approval procedure and help them convert a barren land to a useful land with efficient use of resources and efficacy.

Contractors are an integral part of doing the construction activities for a developer. For a contractor to deliver a sophisticated building in less time and with good quality of work, the developer needs to pay a premium price for the work done by the contractor. The Contractor needs to bring in with him a good amount of workforce, best technologies available to him within his budget, and work as per the schedule provided by the Developer. The price taken by the contractor can vary from time to time as by working in various sites, he would have gained some knowledge for which he quotes a price to it. Both the developer and contractor need to be on the same page to achieve great results in the mere future.

CHAPTER 3

CONSUMER PROTECTION ACT

The new Consumer Protection Act 2019 seeks to revamp the administration and settlement of consumer disputes, with strict penalties, including jail term for adulteration and misleading ads by firms.

The bill, among other things, proposes the setting up of a Central Consumer Protection Authority (CCPA) to promote, protect and enforce the rights of consumers as a class. The CCPA would make interventions to prevent consumer detriment arising from unfair trade practices. The agency can also initiate class action, including enforcing recall, refund and return of products. The Bill also envisages a simplified dispute resolution process, has provision for Mediation and e-filing of cases. The Consumer will be able to file cases in the nearest commission under the jurisdiction he resides. Consumers can file complaints from anywhere and they do not need to hire a lawyer to represent their cases. For mediation, there will be a strict timeline fixed in the rules. Let us dive more deeply into the Act.

Q1. What are the reasons for the necessity of Consumer Protection in the Real-Estate Industry?

Ans: There are three reasons for the necessity of Consumer Protection in the real estate industry. They are as follows:

- The Real Estate Business involves a large amount of money. Therefore, malpractices against consumers would result in large amounts of losses for them. On the other hand, consumer protection would benefit enormously to consumers and is in their best interests and other agents tied to the industry.

- Real estate agents control the Real Estate Industry. When governments formulate policies to improve the real estate industry, they ask people who represent real estate agents. They rarely ask people who represent consumers.

- Consumers lack knowledge. Lack of knowledge and information on the part of consumers about the industry also causes them to be exploited. They are misinformed, cheated, and often lose large amounts of money at the hands of fraud agents because of such a lack of information.

Q2. What are the existing legislation for consumer protection in Real-Estate Sector?

Ans: The existing legislation for consumer protection in Real-Estate Sector are as follows:

- Consumer Protection Act
- Indian Contract Act
- Real Estate Regulation Act
- Competition Act

Q3. Why Consumer Protection Act came into the picture?

Ans: Consumer protection act is a beautiful piece of legislation bought in by our legislature. It also provides speedy redressal of the disputes a consumer's faces. Its major objective is to protect and promote the rights of a consumer. Some of them are as follows:

1. The right to be protected against marketing of goods which are hazardous to life and property;

2. The right to be informed about the quality, quantity, potency, purity, standard and price of goods to protect the consumer against unfair trade practices;

3. The right to be assured, wherever possible, access to an authority of goods at competitive prices;

4. The right to be heard and to be assured that consumers interests will receive due consideration at appropriate forums;

5. The right to seek redressal against unfair trade practices or unscrupulous exploitation of consumers; and

6. The right to consumer education.

Q4. Discuss the landmark case of Belaire Owner's Association vs DLF Ltd case?

Ans: The Competition Commission Of India held that The absence of any single sectoral regulator to regulate the real estate sector in totality, to ensure adoption of transparent and ethical business practices and protect the consumers, has only made the situation in the real estate sector worse. Various sector-specific studies have also brought out that the very establishment of a regulatory mechanism is likely to infuse more investments in the sector, the absence of which has kept investors at bay. Thus, it can be perceived that there has been a crying need for a real estate regulator to ensure transparency and fix accountability. With the high level of vulnerability and risk involved, and with the lack of a regulatory framework, it becomes necessary to extend to the consumers legal protection against the malpractices by real estate agents.

Q5. Discuss the housing construction in the purview of Service definition under the Act?

Ans: The housing construction came under the purview of Service definition under the Act by an ordinance. Now the definition of service has a broader meaning than before. Construction of a house or a flat can be achieved by a person either by doing it himself or by hiring services of a builder or contractor and the same is purchased for consideration. This whole thing comes under the purview of services.

Q6. Discuss the landmark judgement passed by the State Commission in the case of S.P. Dhavaskar vs Housing Commissioner, Karnataka Housing Board?

Ans: the complainant had deposited Rs. 1.66 lakhs with the Housing Board for a house proposed to be built by the Board. He was told that the construction would be completed within two years. Later he was informed that the construction was not up to the expected level because of the use of low-cost technology and that the houses constructed developed distress and might not long and suggested that the complainant might take back the amount of deposit without interest or opt for a new house in place of the house already allotted. The State Commission held that the act of the Housing Board amounted to a deficiency in service and returning Housing and Consumer deposit amount without interest was unreasonable and ordered payment of interest at 18 per cent pa. In appeal, the National Commission upheld the order of the State Commission.

Q7. What are the three consumer disputes redressal Agencies under the act?

Ans: There are three consumer disputes redressal agencies under the Act. They are:

1. District Commission
2. State Commission
3. National Commission

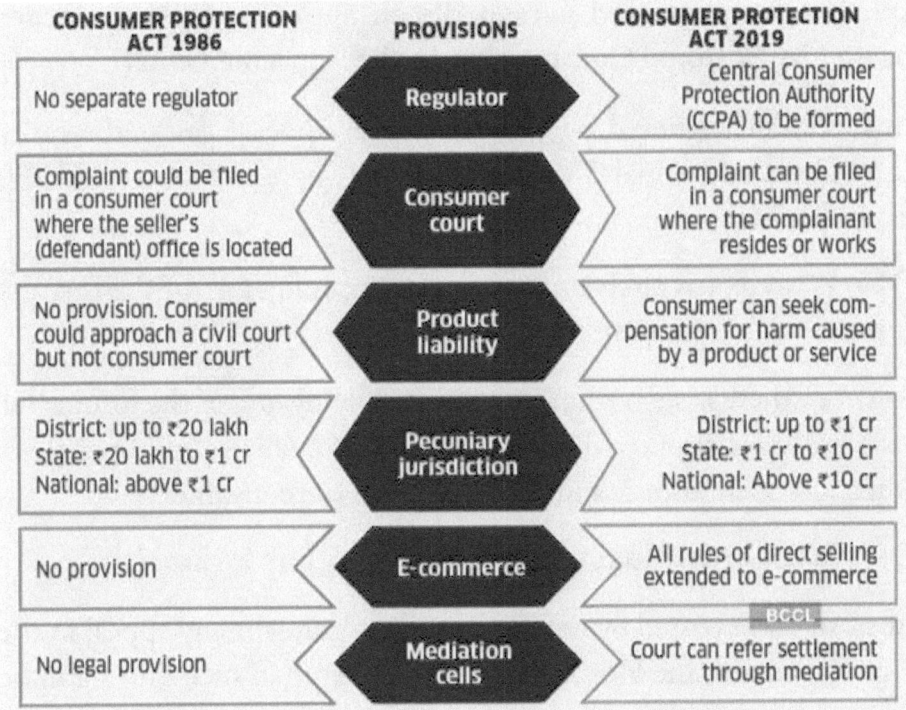

Q8. What is the remedy who came up with an allegation for deficiency in service?

Ans: In the landmark judgement of Tamil Nadu Housing Board vs Sea Shore Apartments Owners Welfare Association, there was an allegation of deficiency in service in housing construction, owing to the demand of additional price by the housing board. The Supreme Court held that the price quoted in the initial advertisement issued for registration of intending purchasers was tentative and since the alteration of the scheme the plinth area and ground area is increased, the demand for the additional price could not be considered to be arbitrary, and hence it was not a deficiency in service.

Q9. Can an aggrieved person file an appeal against the order passed by National Commission in the Supreme Court?

Ans: Yes, an aggrieved person can file an appeal against the order passed by the National Commission in the Supreme Court within 30 days after such orders have been passed.

Q10. Is there any such limitation for applying any of the forums for any consumer disputes?

Ans: Yes, there is such a limitation for applying any of the forums for any consumer disputes. The complaint shall be filed within two years when any such dispute caused damages to the consumer.

Q11. Is the order final which is passed by any forums?

Ans: An order passed by any forums if not gone for any appeal in the higher forum or the Hon'ble Supreme Court than such orders can be deemed to be final.

Q12. Describe the consumer in the real estate sector?

Ans: The term Consumer is described in section 2{d} of the consumer protection Act.

The consumer of the real estate sector for redressal of grievances is only protected by the general consumer protection laws in the country as The Consumer Protection Act.

Q13. Describe the Penalties mentioned under the Act?

Ans: The penalties for false or misleading advertisement as mentioned under the act are as follows:

1. Imprisonment shall not be less than a month and may extend up to 2 years.

2. Fine imposed may extend up to ten lakh rupees, &for every subsequent offence-

- Imprisonment which may extend up to 5 years & fine which may extend up to Rs. 50lakhs.

Q14. Discuss the appeal against orders passed by different forums under the Act (Sec 27A)?

Ans: An aggrieved party can file an appeal against the order which he might feel inappropriate can apply to appeal against the order in the higher forum within 30 days of passing the order.

Q15. Discuss Product Liability under Consumer Protection Act?

Ans: A product liability action against a product manufacturer/ product service provider for any harm caused to him on account of a defective product.

Q16. Discuss the liability of the Product Manufacturer?

Ans: The Product manufacturer will be liable in a product liability action if:

- The product contains some sort of manufacturing defect
- the product has a faulty design
- the product does not conform to the express warranty
- There is some sort of deviation from manufacturing specifications.

CHAPTER 4

SECURITISATION AND RECONSTRUCTION OF FINANCIAL ASSETS AND ENFORCEMENT OF SECURITY INTEREST (SARFAESI) ACT

A brief overview of the (SARFAESI) Act in the context of loan foreclosure and the disposition of assets pledged to obtain those loans.

A loan is a simple transaction in which a borrower borrows money and a lender advances it while collecting interest and this arrangement continues until the borrower repays the loan.

In practice, however, it is observed that there are defaulters and they ruin the lender's financials. While in case of secured loans, the borrower offers collateral such as real estate or machinery which serves as a security to the lender, authorising it to seize and in the event that the borrower defaults on the loan, the lender will sell the asset to recoup its funds.. When a borrower defaults on a loan, the asset is classified as a non-performing asset (NPA).

The Securitisation and Reconstruction of Financial Assets and Enforcement of Security Interest (SARFAESI) Act was enacted to provide a structured forum for the banking sector to manage its mounting NPA stocks and keep up with foreign financial institutions. It allows banks and financial institutions (FIs) to take ownership of securities and sell them. According to the Act, it has "allowed banks and financial institutions to realise long-term assets, manage liquidity problems, asset-liability mismatches, and improve recovery by taking possession of securities, selling them, and reducing nonperforming assets (NPAs) by introducing recovery or reconstruction steps."

The SARFAESI Act's key goal is to make it easier to enforce security interests, i.e. claiming the properties pledged as security for a loan. In the case of a borrower's default, the Act allows the lender to send a demand notice to the defaulting borrower and guarantor, requiring them to pay their debts within 60 days of obtaining the notice in full. If the borrower does not comply with the notice, the bank or financial institution may seize the security or sell, lease, or transfer the security's rights.

Q1. What is Securitisation?

Ans: The process of pooling and repackaging financial assets into marketable securities that can be sold to investors is known as securitisation.

Concerning bad asset management, securitization is the process of conversion of existing loans into marketable securities. The securitization firm is in charge of the loan taker's underlying mortgaged properties.

It can initiate the following steps:

i. Acquisition of financial assets from an originator (bank), and

ii. Obtaining funds from interested institutional investors by issuing security receipts (for raising funds) in order to purchase financial assets or

iii. Funds can be raised in any way that is prescribed, and

iv. Taking possession of mortgaged property, buildings, and other properties can be combined with the acquisition of financial assets.

Q2. What is asset reconstruction?

Ans: Asset reconstruction is the process of converting a non-performing asset into a performing asset.

The asset reconstruction process includes the acquisition of a bad asset by a dedicated asset reconstruction company (ARC), as well as the underlying hypothecated asset, the financing of the bad asset conversion into a good asset using bonds, debentures, securities, and currency, and the realisation of returns from the hypothecated assets.

Reconstruction is done by taking into account all RBI regulations and the SARFAESI Act gives the following components for a reconstruction of assets: –

a. holding control of the borrower's business or modifying the management of the borrower's business,

b. the sale or lease of a portion or all of the borrower's company;

c. rescheduling the repayment of the borrower's debts;

d. enforcement of security interest following the provisions of this Act;

e. repayment of the borrower's obligations;

f. taking possession of secured assets following the provisions of this Act.

Q3. What is meant by 'enforcement of security interests?

Ans: The SARFESI Act empowers the banker. In case the borrower defaults, the banker will issue notice to the defaulting borrower and guarantor to repay the debt within 60 days from the date of the notice. If the borrower fails to comply with the notice, the bank or the financial institution may enforce security interests by following the provisions of the Act:

a. Take possession of the security;

b. The right to sell, lease, or grant the security is sold, leased, or assigned;

c. Appoint Manager to manage the security;

d. Demand that all of the borrower's debtors pay any amount owed to the borrower.

If there are more than one secured creditors, the decision about the enforcement of SARFEASI provisions will be applicable only if 75% of them are agreeing.

Q4. What assets are covered under SARFAESI?

Ans: Any asset, movable or immovable, given as security whether by way of mortgage, hypothecation, or creation of a security interest in any other form except those excluded u/s 31 of the Act.

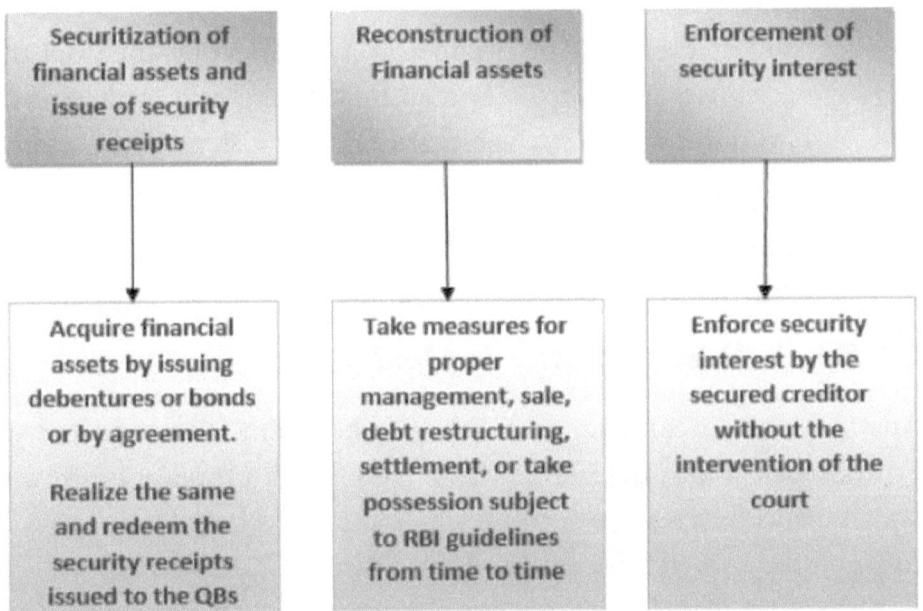

Q5. When do properties fall under this Act?

Ans: Only consider registered assets since it is difficult to obtain information of unpaid liabilities for unregistered properties. If they don't, banks declare the loan a nonperforming asset (NPA) and sell it at auction to recoup the debt.

Q6. Explain the process of securitisation.

Ans: Securitisation is the process of issuing marketable securities backed by the secured assets. Assets are sold after they have been converted into securities. This process involves 3 steps-

1. Identification Process- in this process, the Banks and Financial institutions that decide to go for securitisation are called 'Originators'. The process of selecting various loans and receivables from asset portfolios to convert them into securities is called Identification Process.

2. Transfer Process- The originators after selecting the pool of assets, pass it on to the Special Purpose Vehicle or the trust. This is by way of a sale agreement; after transferring the assets, the originators removing them from balance sheets.

3. Issuing Securities- the SPV then convertors the assets to securities. It will be provided to investors.

Q7. How is the auction price decided?

Ans: Auction Price depends on the market value of the property. Professional valuers determine the value of such property based on which banks fix a reserve or minimum bid price. The valuations tend to be on the conservative side as it is a distressed sale.

The excess sum is issued to the borrower if the price fetched exceeds the bank's dues.

Q8. How do I participate in the auction?

Ans: Here is the step by step process of how the auction process is conducted and what you are supposed to do. Intending bidders can inspect the property before the date of auction and get authorisation from the chief manager. Once made up mind to buy the property the following procedures to be followed.

Step1:- Read the notification thoroughly and need to use the date, time, place and process. Write down the reserve price, EMD, inspection date, time, and location of the auction.

Please make sure where you collect the Tender form, with the date and time and last date of submission.

Step2:- Collect a tender form from the given place and time

Step3:- Buy a DD of EMD amount (Ranges from 10 % to 25% of Reserve Price).

Step4:- You have to submit DD along with a filled-in Tender form before the due date/time along with any ID proof as mentioned (PAN card / Address proof etc.)

Now you have completed all formalities related to the auction and you are one of the eligible bidders.

In the next step, the authorised officer concern to start the bidding process at the reserve price.

In the next step, if you are interested and you can raise your bid if you are a successful bidder, you have to deposit between 25% to 30% bid amount inclusive of EMD at the bank on the same day. Remaining balance within 45 days. Banks can guarantee you more time in some cases.. The total amount deposited by the bidder will be forfeited if the balance is not paid within the specified time frame, and the property will be resold. The forfeited bidder loses all rights to the land.

Q9. What are the features of the amendment to the SARFAESI Act in 2016?

Ans: In August 2016, the government amended the SARFAESI Act to empower Asset Reconstruction Companies (ARCs), revitalise Debt Recovery Tribunals (DRTs), and improve asset reconstruction effectiveness under the current bankruptcy law.

The RBI now has more regulatory authority over the operation of ARCs as a result of the amendment. In the light of the newly enacted bankruptcy legislation, it was also intended to empower asset restoration and the operation of DRTs.

The purpose of the register, which includes a central database of all loans against properties made by all lenders, has been expanded to provide more details as a result of the amendment.

The RBI will be given more authority to audit and inspect ARCs, as well as the ability to suspend the chairman and any other manager. It can also appoint central bank officials to the boards of ARCs. Here RBI gets the power to impose certain penalties on such ARC's. The penalty amount has been increased from Rs 5 lakhs to Rs 1 crore.

The SARFAESI Act now covers hire purchase and financial leases, thanks to the change. The amendment aims to make DRT procedures more effective. Online protocols will be implemented, including the electronic filing of recovery applications, records, and written statements.

The amendments are essential for DRTs as they can play an essential role under the new Bankruptcy law. DRTs will be the cornerstone of the bankruptcy code, dealing with all individual insolvency proceedings. Until filing an appeal at a DRT, the defaulter must deposit 50% of the debt due.

Q10. Whether Authorised Officer can straight away go to the borrower and take physical possession of the secured asset without the help of the Judicial Magistrate or District Magistrate?

Ans: In certain cases, though, it is possible. However, it is advisable to file an application under Section 14 of the Act, and court officers may proceed to the site until the Magistrate issues an order. They take physical custody of the protected asset themselves with the assistance of the police, and the recovered charged property is then handed over to the Approved Officer by the court officer. Hence, through physical possession is taken by the Court Officer, the Authorized Officer of the Bank must be physically present at the site while taking over any of the Bank's assets, as directed by the Magistrate.

Q11. Why does Bank Auction secure Assets?

Ans: When a bank grants a loan to a borrower, they usually obtain a security interest from a borrower who pledges an asset to secure the loan. Suppose the borrower defaults on the loan, the bank takes possession of the secured asset and sells it to recover the amount due from the borrower after observing / compliance with all legal formalities.

Q12. What are the pros and cons of such buys?

Ans: Typically, these properties are 20-30 per cent cheaper than the market price. Also, since the bank had previously lent against the property, there is clarity on the property title. These properties, on the other hand, are being sold "as is." There may be outstanding debts or even legal proceedings. Until carefully examined, these liabilities will be automatically transferred to you.

Checklist before buying a property

To preclude future disputes, follow the checklist given below:

a. Examine the original sale deed and use Central Registry of Securitisation Asset Reconstruction and Security Interest (CERSAI) records to ensure that the property is free from other bank liabilities or loans. Only consider registered assets since details on unpaid liabilities for unregistered assets are difficult to come by.

b. Read the bid document carefully to learn about the legal title and who is responsible for any outstanding dues. This will assist you in determining the property's exact liability.

c. By auctioning the property, the bank does not turn into the owner. Hire a lawyer to investigate and validate the ownership of the title. This may add to the cost but will clarify ownership.

d. Before continuing with the property sale, find out if the lender has received a Recovery Certificate from the Debt Recovery Tribunal (DRT).

e. The bank must issue an Indemnity Certificate to protect you from the risk of future claims by the owner. If necessary, request that the owner serve as the transaction's verifying party.

f. The lender should obtain a No Objection Certificate (NOC) from the appropriate housing society, if applicable. Examine previous utility bills, ongoing lawsuits, and other contractual obligations.

g. When you buy a property worth more than 50 lakhs, you are required to deduct 1% tax at the source, i.e., credit TDS to the PAN of the original owner. Ask the bank to treat the TDS as a part of the purchase.

h. To protect yourself against the seller backing out of the transaction, request the inclusion of an appropriate penalty clause.

In terms of the requisite diligence, purchasing a distressed property necessitates patience and perseverance. Follow through with the above checklist and you will be rewarded with one of the most gratifying and fulfilling financial decisions of your life.

Q13. Any remedies for defect or deficiency of services under the Consumer Act?

Ans: When you buy a property from a developer and find that the quality of construction is not promised initially, you can file a case against the developer in the consumer court, asking for compensation.

If you buy a house at auction, you won't be able to use this remedy.

A buyer cannot approach a consumer court in such cases. The buyer would not count as a 'consumer' since there is no 'sale' of products and services.'

Auctioned properties can appeal to you because they are usually available at a discount, but they are not without risk. So, before bidding on one, make sure you've done your homework. Use the services of a lawyer if necessary.

The Act, to insulate assets legally, addresses the financial assets of banks and other secured creditors. Financial institutions have the authority and power to deal with various forms of bad assets under the act's various provisions. The main objectives of the SARFAESI Act under Indian insolvency law are as follows:

- The Act details the procedures for NPAs' transfer to the asset reconstruction companies for asset reconstruction.

- The Act establishes the legal structure in India for scanning activities.

- The Act gives financial institutions the authority to seize charged or hypothecated immovable property in order to recover debts.

- The Act imposes the security interest without the need for court intervention.

CHAPTER 5

FEMA

The Foreign Exchange Management Act, 1999 (FEMA) was introduced in India to facilitate foreign trade and international payments. In addition to this, FEMA was designed to assist in the orderly development and maintenance of the Indian Foreign Exchange (Forex) Market. FEMA outlines the framework for dealing with all Foreign Exchange transactions in the country.

Foreign Exchange transactions have been classified into two categories:

- Capital Account Transactions, and
- Current Account Transactions.

Capital Account Transactions arise from the movement of capital in the economy through Capital Receipts and Expenditures. Capital Account recognises the domestic investment in foreign assets and foreign investment in domestic ones.

Current Account Transactions are those transactions that involve inflow and outflow of money to and from the country/countries during a year due to the trading or rendering of commodities, services, and incomes. The health of the Current Account is an effective indicator of the status of an economy.

Q1. Which laws and regulations govern Foreign Investment in India?

Ans: Foreign investment in India is regulated under the provisions of the Foreign Exchange Management Act (FEMA), 1999, and the

Foreign Exchange Management (Transfer or Issue of a Security by a Person resident outside India) Regulations, 2017.

FEMA was enacted to consolidate the laws relating to the management of Foreign Exchange to facilitate foreign trade and payments and promote the development and maintenance of the Foreign Exchange (Forex) Market in India.

Based on the type of entity one proposes to incorporate, compliance with other legislation such as the Foreign Exchange Management (Establishment in India of a Branch office or a liaison office or a project office or any other place of business) Regulations, 2016 is also necessary.

Q2. What constitutes 'Foreign Investment' under Indian Law?

Ans: 'Foreign Investment' is an investment made in the capital instruments of an Indian company or the equity capital of a Limited Liability Partnership (LLP) by a person resident outside India on a repatriable basis.

Q3. Who is a "Person Resident Outside India"?

Ans: A "Person Resident outside India" refers to a person who is not a resident in India. The term can be understood better if the definition of "Person Resident in India" is clear. A "Person Resident in India" is:

i. A person residing in India for more than 182 days during the preceding financial year but does not include

   a. A person who has gone out of India or who stays outside India, in either case:

   - For or on taking up employment outside India
   - For carrying on outside India a business or vocation outside India

- For any other purpose in such circumstances as would indicate his intention to stay outside India for an uncertain period

b. A person who has come to or stays in India, in either case, otherwise than

- For or on taking up employment in India
- For carrying on in India a business or vocation in India
- For any other purpose, in such circumstances, it would indicate his intention to stay in India for an uncertain period

iii. Any person or body corporate registered or incorporated in India

iv. An office, Branch, or agency in India owned or controlled by a person resident outside India

v. An office, agency, or Branch outside India owned or controlled by a person resident in India

Q4. What are the capital instruments through which foreign investment may be affected?

Ans: A foreign investor may make investments in eligible Indian entities in various instruments such as Equity Shares, Debentures, Preference Shares, and Share Warrants issued under the regulations of the Securities and Exchange Board of India (SEBI). Capital instruments are subject to a minimum lock-in period of 1 year or as prescribed for the specific sector, whichever is higher. Note that there is no Option or Right to exit at an assured price.

Q5. Is foreign investment allowed in all sectors?

Ans: No, FEMA prescribes a list of sectors where foreign investment is prohibited.

These are:

i. Lottery Business, including Government/private lottery, online lotteries, etc.

ii. Betting and Gambling including casinos

iii. Chit funds

iv. Nidhi companies

v. Trading in Transferable Development Rights (TDRs)

vi. Real Estate

vii. Manufacturing of cigars, cigarillos, cigarettes, and cheroots of tobacco or tobacco substitutes

viii. Sectors not open to private sector investment such as Railways, Atomic Energy, etc.

Q6. Barring the sectoral prohibition, can foreign investments be made in all other sectors? What is the limit on the amount of investment in various sectors?

Ans: The FEMA and the Foreign Direct Investment Policy prescribe certain limits on FDI in each sector. The Foreign Investors need to comply with such prescribed limits and the corresponding applicable conditions.

The following is the limit of FDI investments in major sectors and the routes through which the investment can be made:

Sector	FDI Limit	Route
Agriculture and Allied Activities	100%	Automatic
Coal Mining	100%	Automatic
Defence	100%	Automatic up to 49%
		Government Beyond 49%
Print Media	26%	Government
Airports	100%	Automatic
Telecom	100%	Automatic up to 49%
		Government Beyond 49%
Single Brand Retail	100%	Automatic up to 49%
		Government Beyond 49%
Private Sector Banks	74%	Automatic up to 49%
		Government Beyond 49%
Public Sector Banks	20%	Government
Insurance and Pension	74%	Automatic

Q7. Are there any additional conditions, including entry conditions that a foreign investor is required to comply with?

Ans: Investment made by non-residents in the capital of a resident entity in certain sectors can be allowed with certain entry conditions. These conditions may include sector-specific norms for lock-in period minimum capitalization, etc. Investors are required to comply with all relevant sectoral laws, regulations, rules, and security conditions.

Q8. What are the entry routes for investment through FDI?

Ans: Non-residents can make investments through 2 routes:

- Automatic Route – where prior regulatory approval is not required

- Government Route – where prior regulatory approval is required

Q9. What is the difference between the Automatic Route and the Government Route?

Ans: Automatic Route- An Indian company subject to prescribed FDI caps, sectoral regulations, and licensing requirements issues capital instruments to persons resident outside India under the Automatic Route. This route does not require prior approval of regulatory and other government bodies.

There are certain sectors in which foreign investment cannot be made via the Automatic Route, and prior approval of regulatory and government authorities is required. Domestic Civil Aviation, Broadcasting, Print and News Media, Mining, and Defence are some prominent examples.

Approval Route – If the investment in a sector is not eligible for the "Automatic Route", the organization in which such foreign investment is proposed to be made would have to submit an application on the Foreign Investment Facilitation Portal for approval.

The approval is provided by the concerned ministry or department at its discretion on a case-to-case basis. While approving an investment proposal, the concerned department or ministry generally takes factors such as flow of Foreign Exchange, overall benefits for the economy, potential and prospects for export, the potential for large-scale employment generation, etc., into consideration.

POSSIBLE ROUTES FOR INVESTMENT

Automatic Route

- Overseas JV/WOS to be engaged in bonafide business activity except real estate and banking;
- Investment in Financial Sector should comply with additional conditions
- Indian party not on RBI's Exporters' Caution List/list of defaulters/under investigation by an Authority such as ED, SEBI etc.
- Overall ceiling of financial commitment in all JV/WOS is 100% of net worth as on last audited Balance Sheet
- Submission of Form Annual Performance Report in respect of all its overseas investment

Approval Route

- Cases not covered under Automatic route
- Specific application to RBI with necessary documents in Form ODI through the AD (Category I Bank) along with prescribed supporting and documents
- RBI would inter alia consider the following factors:
  ○ Prima facie viability of JV/WOS outside India
  ○ Contribution to external trade and other benefits
  - which will accrue to India through such investment
  ○ Financial position and business track record of the
  - Indian party and foreign entity
  ○ Expertise and experience of the Indian party in the
  - same or related line of activity of the JV/WOS outside India.

Q10. What are the different forms in which a foreign entity can establish its presence in India?

Ans: Depending on the proposed activities of such foreign entity, a foreign entity can establish its presence in India, either through the opening of 3 types of establishments:

- Liaison Office
- Project Office
- Branch Office

The foreign entity can also directly investing in an Indian company, a Partnership Firm, or a Limited Liability Partnership (LLP).

Q11. What is the difference between a Liaison Office, Branch Office, and Project Office?

Ans: Liaison Office acts as a communication channel between the principal place of business or head office and entities in India. The Liaison Office neither directly nor indirectly indulges in any commercial, trading, or industrial activity and maintains itself out of the inflow of remittances received through legal banking channels.

Branch Office is any establishment described as such by the company and is used for day-to-day operations.

A Project Office represents a foreign company carrying out a project in India but does not include a Liaison Office.

Q12. What are the eligibility criteria for establishing the Liaison Office, Branch Office, and Project Office?

Ans: For establishing a Liaison Office, the foreign entity must demonstrate a profitable track record during the immediately preceding 3 financial years in its home country and a Net Worth of at least USD 50,000, or its equivalent.

To set up a Branch Office, the foreign entity must demonstrate a profitable track record during the immediately preceding 3 financial years in its home country and a Net Worth of at least USD 1,00,000, or it is equivalent.

For setting up a Project Office, the foreign entity must have entered into a legal contract with an Indian company for executing a project in India. The project should be directly or indirectly funded by the inflow of remittances, a bilateral or multilateral International financing agency, or a term loan lent by an Indian bank.

Liaison Office

Q13. Is prior Reserve Bank of India (RBI) approval required for setting up of Liaison Office?

Ans: Yes, prior RBI approval is required for setting up a Liaison Office.

Q14. What is the validity of the above approval?

Ans: The above approval is valid for 3 years. The 3 years may be extended for 3 years from the date of expiry of the original approval or extension granted, subject to such directions issued by the RBI in this regard.

Q15. What is the Procedure for Application of a Liaison Office?

Ans: Application to set up a Liaison Office has to be made to the RBI in the prescribed Form FNC and the relevant documentation through an AD Category – I Bank identified by the applicant they intend to pursue banking relations. The following documents need to be attached along with Form FNC:

i. A Cover Letter to the FNC Form mentioning the details of the activities of the head office, and its operations across the world, number of employees globally, its history of presence, if any, in India, etc.;

ii. English version of the Certificate of Incorporation/ Registration, or Memorandum and Articles of Association attested by the Indian Embassy or a Notary

iii. Balance Sheet of the applicant company of the last 5 years

iv. Banker's Report from the banker of the applicant in the host country showing the time that the applicant has had banking relations with the concerned bank

v. A Letter of Comfort provided by the parent company

vi. Power of Attorney in favour of the signatory of FNC Form in case the head of the overseas entity is not signing the FNC form

Besides, promotional literature and other similar materials are also attached with the application by the applicant

Q16. Is there any compliance applicable to the Liaison Office?

Ans: Yes, the regulations have prescribed a set of compliances that each Liaison Office is permitted to make:

i. The Liaison Office must conduct an audit of its accounts and file their performance reports with the RBI. LO has to file, on or before September 30 each year, an 'Annual Activity Certificate' as at the end of March 31st along with the audited financial statements including the accounts of receipt and payment the Authorized Dealer with a copy marked to the Directorate-General of Income Tax (International Taxation), New Delhi

ii. The Liaison Office has to carry out certain statutory filings under the Companies Act, 2013 and comply with other requirements of local law, including Central and State labour legislations

iii. Liaison Office is allowed to open non-interest-bearing current accounts in India. Such offices are required to approach Indian banks for opening accounts with them

iv. Liaison Office is required to register with the Registrar of Companies, if required as per the Companies Act, 2013

v. Liaison Office is required to obtain Permanent Account the Number from the Income Tax Authorities post the setting up of the office and is required to report the same in the Annual Activity Certificate

vi. All Liaison offices have to carry out incidental activities from lease property subject to lease period not exceeding 5 years

Branch Office

Q17. Is prior RBI approval required for setting up of Branch Office?

Ans: Yes, prior RBI approval is required for setting up of Branch Office.

Q18. What is the procedure for the application of a Branch Office?

Ans: Permission to set up a Branch Office has to be made to the RBI, through an Authorized Dealer, in the prescribed Form FNC along with the relevant documentation. The documents required to be attached the following:

- It sets out the details concerning the activities of the head office and its worldwide operations, number of employees worldwide, financial strength, reputation, its previous presence, if any, in India, etc.

- An English version of the Documents attested by the Indian Embassy/Notary Public in the country of registration

- The audited the balance sheet of the applicant company/firm for the last 3 years

- Banker's report from the applicant's banker in the host country/country of registration showing the number of years that the applicant has had banking relations with that bank

- A Letter of Comfort from the parent company, in the prescribed form, if required

- Promotional literature of the applicant is also normally attached to the application.

Q19. What is the permitted scope of activities for a Branch Office?

Ans: The following activities are permitted to be undertaken by a Branch Office in India under the Regulations:

- To carry on export/import of goods (procurement of goods for export and sale of goods after the import is allowed only on a wholesale basis)

- To render professional or consultancy services

- To conduct research work in India in which the parent company is engaged

- To promote technical and/or financial collaborations between Indian companies and a parent or overseas group companies

- To represent the parent company and other foreign companies in various matters in India

- To render services in information technology and development of software in India

- To provide technical support to the products supplied by the companies of the parent/group

- To set up a foreign airline/shipping company

Project Office

Q20. Is prior RBI approval required for setting up of Project Office?

Ans: No, prior RBI approval is not required in case if a project has been awarded in India to such a foreign company.

Q21. What is the validity of the Project Office?

Ans: The validity to the Project Office is granted for the duration of the project.

Q22. What is the permitted scope of activities for a Project Office?

Ans: The Project Office can be set up for the sole purpose of executing the project and cannot undertake any other activities.

The Companies Act

Company

Q1. What is a Company?

Ans: An Indian Company is a company incorporated under the Companies Act 2013, or under any previous company law. A foreign entity, subject to a sectoral cap, invests in a company incorporated under the Companies Act 2013 through either of the following vehicles:

- Wholly Owned Subsidiary
- Joint Venture Company where it may partner with another foreign or Indian company for expertise in technology, financial resources, etc.

Q2. What is the procedure for FDI in a company?

Ans: FDI can be brought into an Indian company either through one of the following options:

i. Incorporation of an Indian company

   A company may issue Equity Shares, Convertible Preference Shares, Convertible Debentures to non-residents under the applicable provisions

ii. Acquisition of existing shares as a way of entry

   Transfer of Equity Shares, or Convertible Debentures of an Indian company from Indian residents or non-residents, by way of sale, does not require prior Government approval provided the following conditions are satisfied

   - The transfer is per the entry routes (as applicable) under the FDI Policy

   - After the transfer, the non-resident shareholding complies with the FDI Policy's sectoral limits.

- The price at which the transfer takes place is greater than or equal to the fair valuation of shares as determined by a Merchant Banker or a Chartered Accountant registered under SEBI as per any internationally accepted valuation methodology. Further, an amount at most 25% of the entire value of the transfer can be paid by the buyer on a deferred basis

LLP

Q3. What is an LLP?

Ans: LLP combines the versatility of a partnership and the benefits of a company's limited liability at a low compliance cost. In other words, it is a corporate business vehicle that provides a corporation with the protection of limited liability. However, it enables its members to organize their internal management based on a mutual agreement, similar to that in a partnership firm. An LLP is governed by the provisions of the Limited Liability Partnership Act, 2008 (LLP Act).

Q4. What are the requirements for the formation of an LLP?

Ans: The requirements for the formation of an LLP:

i. An LLP can be incorporated with two partners who can be individuals or corporates. Further, for incorporating an LLP, there need to be at least 2 'Designated Partners', of which at least one must be an Indian resident

ii. To register for an Indian LLP, an applicant needs to apply for a Director's Identification Number (DIN), which can be done by filing an e-Form. The Digital Signature Certificate (DSC) must be obtained by the applicant. After that, the applicant needs to approve by the Ministry of Corporate Affairs. Once the name is approved, the foreign company can register the LLP by filing the incorporation form.

Q5. Can FDI be invested in an LLP?

Ans: FDI is permitted under the automatic route, only in LLPs operating in sectors/activities where 100% (one hundred percent) FDI is allowed through the automatic route and there are no FDI-linked performance conditions. Moreover, an LLP can convert to a corporation. Similarly, the automated route now allows for the conversion of corporation into an LLP.

Partnership Firm

Q6. What is a Partnership Firm?

Ans: A partnership is described as a relationship between two or more people who have decided to split the profits from a company they are both involved in or any of them acting for all. The owners in the partnership business the individually known as the "partners" and collectively known as a "firm". It is formed through an agreement, which may be either written or oral. "Partnership Deed" refers to a formal document that has been properly stamped and registered. In certain instances, the Partnership Deed sets out the rights, responsibilities, and obligations of the partners. However, when the Partnership Deed does not specify the rights and obligations, the provisions of the Indian Partnership Act, 1932 (Partnership Act) will apply.

Q7. What are the requirements for the formation of a Partnership Firm?

Ans: A Partnership Firm may be registered by applying with the Registrar of Firms of the area in which any firm's business is situated or proposed to be situated. The application shall contain:

- The firm's name
- The location of a company's headquarters or principal place of business
- Names of the other locations where the company does business
- Date of joining of each partner
- Partners' names in their absolute and permanent addresses
- Firm's duration

Q8. Can FDI be made in a Partnership Firm?

Ans: Foreign direct investment (FDI) is permitted in partnership companies, subject to the following conditions.:

i. If a firm or a proprietorship is situated in India, an NRI or a PIO residing abroad may invest in the capital of that firm on a non-repatriation basis:
   - Amount is deposited by inward remittance or from an NRE, FCNR(B) or NRO account with approved dealers or banks.

- The partnership firm does not work in the agricultural/plantation, real estate, or print media industries.
- The amount invested would not be able to be repatriated outside of India.

ii. NRIs/PIO may seek prior permission of RBI for investment in partnership firms with a Repatriation Option. RBI processes the application after consulting with the government

iii. Investment by non-residents other than NRIs/PIO: A person resident outside India other than NRIs/PIO may make an application and seek prior approval of the RBI for investing the capital of a partnership firm in India. The government will be consulted before making a decision on the application.

iv. Restrictions: A NRI or PIO is not permitted to invest in a company or sole proprietorship engaged in agricultural/plantation activities, real estate, or print media.

CHAPTER 6

MRTP ACT

The Maharashtra Regional Town planning Act started as the Bombay Act, 1915 which provided for the following

1. Preparation of town planning schemes
2. Recovery of betterment contribution from benefitted owners of Planning Act, 1954 which brought forward the following

    - Concept of Development plan and
    - Town planning remained the main instrument for the implementation of Land

But has the following shortcoming that it has piecemeal planning, i.e. no consideration given to the adjoining areas

Thus, the Bombay Act, 1915 was replaced by the Bombay Town

of Development planning schemes

However, the Concept of "Regional Planning" was realized in the Maharashtra Regional Town Planning Act of 1966 which

- Regulated Development in the urban areas
- And in the areas that have the potential of being urbanized

Q1. Who are the participants in the MRTP Act?

Ans: The participants in the MRTP Act are:

   i. The Regional Planning Board consists- The director of town planning, town planning officer, others appointed by the State local authorities, and other persons with special knowledge or practical experience.

ii. The Regional planning committee- Advisory body.

iii. Planning Authority- both Local and Special planning authority.

iv. State Government.

v. Public.

Q2. What are the Objectives of the MRTP Act?

Ans: Objectives of the enactment of the MRTP Act are:

- Planning Development in "Regions."
- Constitution of Regional Planning Boards.
- Better provisions for preparation of Development Planning and Town planning.
- To provide for the creations of new towns.
- To make provisions for the Compulsory Acquisition of land for public purposes in respect of the plans.

Q3. What are the Salient Features of the MRTP Act?

Ans: The salient features of the MRTP Act are:

- Provisions for Regional Planning, Development Planning & Town Planning.
- Implementation schemes: Land accent., TDR, Plot reconstitution.
- This act also provides for finance, accounting, auditing, and governance for plan enforcement.

Q4. What are the scales of the MRTP Act?

i. Regional Plan.

ii. Development plan.

iii. Town Planning Scheme.

Q5. What are the regional planning contents & scale?

Ans: Regional planning contents and scale are:
- Allocation of land for different uses.
- Reservation of areas for open spaces, recreation, etc.
- Transport & communication.
- Water supply, irrigation, and other public services and facilities.
- Greenfield construction areas are being reserved.
- Natural scenery, woodland, and other areas are preserved, conserved, and created.
- Preservation of the past.
- Military and defence-related areas.
- Erosion control, afforestation, reforestation, and other environmental concerns.
- Irrigation, water management, flood control, and other proposals.
- Distribution of population.

Q6. What is the process for a regional plan under MRTP Act?

i. Establishment of the region:- The State Government does it through a notification in official; gazette.

ii. Constitution of regional planning board: – this is done by the State Government, through a notification in the official gazette.

iii. Survey of the region:- The regional planning board does this and there is no such prescribed time limit, but as the state government may determine.

iv. Preparation of draft regional plan:- The regional planning board does the draft regional plan through a notification in the official gazette, copies available for sale to public objections & suggestions invited before the date not less than four months.

v. Modifications: the regional planning committee performs modification. The reasonable opportunity to all persons affected of being heard.

vi. Submissions to state government:- By the regional planning board.

vii. Publication of 'final regional plan' & date of operation:- By the State Government, available for sale to public plan would into operation, not before 60 days from publication restriction on change of user or development.

viii. Revision of regional plan:- By state government, not earlier than 10 years may follow the same process right from the region's establishment.

Q7. What are the contents and scale of the development plan?

Ans: The contents and scale of development plans are:
- Allocation of land for different uses.
- Reservation of areas for open spaces, recreation, etc.
- Transport & communication

- Public utilities & amenities like water supply, drainage, etc.
- Services industries, industrial estates. etc.
- Preservation, conservation & development of areas of natural scenery, forest, etc.
- Heritage preservation
- Proposals for irrigation, water supply, flood control, etc.
- The filling up or reclamation of low-lying, swampy, or unhealthy areas or levelling up of land.
- Development control regulations.

Q8. What is the process of the Development Plan?

Ans: The processes of the Development Plan are:

i. Declaration of the intention to prepare the DP:- planning authority through a notification in the official gazette and restriction on development. Suggestions and objections invited from the public, not before 60 days.

ii. Survey and preparation of existing land-use map:- this step is done by the planning authority, not later than 6 months from the date of declaration of intention. The State Government can extend time.

iii. Preparation of draft development plan:- planning authority should draft a development plan not later than 24 months from the declaration of intention and such notification in the official gazette. Within 60 days, suggestions and objections are invited from notification.

iv. Modification in the draft DP: The planning committee will give a reasonable opportunity to be heard to the affected party and submit a report to the planning authority within 2 months, including modifications in draft DP within 3months of receipt from PC and such notification in the Official gazette.

v. Suggestions & objections invited from the public:- within 60 days from the date of the notice.

vi. Submission to the state government:- within 12 months from the date of publication of notice in the official gazette regarding its preparation. It may be extended but not more than 24 months.

vii. Sanction of the plan:- state government within 12 months from the date of receipt of the plan and such notification in the official gazette. The objections will be allowed within 60 days.

viii. Final development plan and acquiring of land:- state government and planning authority provide final development plan into operation after 1 month from its publication. It acquiring of land within 20 years from the date of operation

Q9. What are the Contents of a Draft Town Planning Scheme?

Ans:

1. Ownership, area, and tenure of original landholdings.
2. Reservation, purchase, or allotment of land information.
3. Dimensions and limits
4. Estimated total costs.
5. Ownership of the final plots is assigned.

Q10. What is the process of the Draft Town Planning Scheme?

Ans: The processes of the Draft Town Planning Scheme are:

i. Declaration of intention:- notification in the official gazette and any suggestions and objections invited from the public within 30 days from the date of the notice.

ii. Preparation & Publication of Draft Scheme:- within 12 months of declaration restriction development.

iii. Appointment of Arbitrator:- this will be done within 1 month of sanction of the draft. For such suggestions and objections are invited.

iv. Submission of Final Scheme to State Govt.

v. Sanction of final TP Scheme:- this step will be done within 4 months of submission.

vi. Enforcement of Scheme.

Q11. What are the shortcomings of the Maharashtra Regional Town Planning Act?

Ans:

- No definite time limit prescribed for the preparation of DP by the planning authority
- Reservations for public use on private lands remain on the paper itself.
- DPs too idealistic, out of implementing capacity.
- Act casts an obligation on the planning authority to prepare a DP, but no similar obligation to implement it.
- No time limit prescribed for TPS.

Q12. What does the planning and development fund consist of?

Ans: The planning and development fund consists of:

1. Grants from National & State Govt. and any other agencies.
2. Budget allocated to the planning authority.
3. Development charges.
4. Betterment charges.
5. Development permission charges.
6. Loans.

Q13. Whether the plan first prepared and notified under Section 21 of the Maharashtra Regional and Town Planning Act, 1966 ('MRTP Act') is the final development plan and The final development plan proposed under Section 21 of the MRTP Act is just a modification of the plan prepared under Section 38?

Ans: Dealing with the question that whether the plan first prepared and notified under Section 21 of the Maharashtra Regional and Town Planning Act, 1966 ('MRTP Act'), Is the final development plan under Section 38 simply a modification of the final development plan proposed under Section 21 of the MRTP Act, necessitating the MRTP Act's Section 127(2) notice is not required and the period of publication of the development plan first notified under Section 21 and not the revised development plan under Section 38 of MRTP Act, a bench of Ranjan Gogoi and R.K. Agrawal, JJ said that under Section 127 of MRTP Act, a notice must be issued by the landowner or any person interested in the land to the authority if no acquisition on the land bought from the owner has been started within ten years of the final development plan coming into effect.

The court further held that after service of the notice, a required period of six months must pass before the authority can take the appropriate action, as represented by Jayant Bhushan and Shekhar Naphade. Only the lapse of the reservation may occur if no acquisition is initiated even after this.

If the owner or someone else fails to give such notice, the reservation, allotment, or land designation under a development plan is presumed to have lapsed. As a result, there is no chance of the property being accessible to the owner for construction or other purposes.

The appellants' notice under Section 127 of the MRTP Act was released just two years after the final revised proposal under Section 38 of the MRTP Act was issued in this case, had come into operation and not the period prescribed from the publication of the final development plan notified under Section 21 of MRTP Act. Prafulla C. Dave v. Municipal Commissioner, decided on 3.12.2014

Q14. Discuss regional plans as mentioned under the act?

Ans: Regional plans are mentioned under sections 13-20 of the MRTP Act. Some of the contents of the regional plans are as follows-

- Allocation of land for different uses and also can be used for residential and industrial purpose,
- Reservation of areas for open spaces,
- Development in multiple areas of infrastructure, etc.

After submitting the regional plan to the respective state government, the state government may approve the regional plan or reject the same. After the approval of the plan by the state govt. the respective state govt. needs to make the publication of the regional plan along with the date of its operation.

Q15. Discuss the developmental plan as discussed under the act?

Ans: The planning Authority needs to carry out a survey and prepare a developmental plan within its area specified and shall submit such plans for approval from the respective state governments. After such application made by the Authority, the govt. will take respective steps to approve/reject the same.

Q16. What modifications can be made by the respective state governments?

Ans: Some of the modifications that the respective state governments can make are as follows-

- Any modification to the proposed site results in a reduction of the area by more than 50%.
- Inserting any new thing to the proposed plan or making slight changes to the proposed plan.
- Changes made in a proposal for the usage of the lands in different zones.
- Any changes made in the floor space index.

Q17. Describe the land acquisition under the MRTP Act.

Ans: It is dealt with under chapter 7 of the MRTP Act. Section 125 deals with the compulsory acquisition of land for the development process under the act. The same is done for a public purpose or comprehensive development purposes.

The Appropriate Authority can acquire the land in the following ways-

- Utilizing an agreement;
- Through the lease;

- Through acquiring land as mentioned in Land Acquisition Act; &Etc.

The respective state government has vested power to acquire land for some other purposes, not stated in the Development Scheme.

CHAPTER 7

LAND ACQUISITION REHABILITATION AND RESETTLEMENT ACT, 2013

The Land Acquisition Rehabilitation and Resettlement Act, 2013 was passed by the Hon'ble Lok Sabha in March 2015. The Right to Fair Compensation and Transparency in Land Acquisition, Rehabilitation, and Resettlement Act of 2013 is the name of the legislation. The act outlines the process for the acquisition of land for public welfare. It provides for bringing transparency into the land acquisition system, giving fair remuneration to landowners, and guiding the government to help rehabilitate those whose land has been acquired.

According to the Act, land can be acquired by the government for:

- Its use
- Public Sector companies, or
- For 'Public Purpose.'

The Act requires a Social Impact Assessment to identify affected families and calculate the social impact when the land is acquired.

Q1. What is included in the 'Public Purpose' for which land can be acquired?

Ans: 'Public Purpose' includes the following uses of land:

- For national or state security, or the use of security services including armed forces under the control of central or state governments.

- For developing public infrastructure, but not private infrastructures like schools and hospitals.
- For a project associated with agriculture and allied activities.
- For manufacturing zones, mining activities, industrial corridors, or other projects mentioned in the National Manufacturing Policy.
- For water conservation, harvesting projects, or for development of village sites.
- For government-owned or aided educational and research institutions.
- For affordable housing and other planned development projects.
- For the development of housing infrastructure for people affected by natural calamities.

Over the past few years, there have been several cases where the definition of 'Public Purpose' was not laid clear by the government. The judiciary has also viewed the 'Public Purpose' clause rather liberally and has upheld the justification given by the government regarding the acquisition of land for 'Public Purpose'. This view of the judiciary was seen in cases like Bajirao Kote vs State of Maharashtra and C. Parekh vs The State of Gujarat.

Nevertheless, in more recent judgments, there has been a shift in the attitude of the judiciary. In Dev Sharan vs State of Uttar Pradesh, the Supreme Court objected to the acquisition of land for the benefit of a particular group of people and compromising the interests of a larger section of people. The apex court called such acquisition as defeating the objectives of 'Public Purpose'.

Q2. Is the consent of landowners required before land acquisition under the Act?

Ans: There are 3 different categories of consent that are provided under the Act:

- When the government acquires the land for 'public purpose', and the government controls the land directly, the consent of landowners is not required

- When the land is acquired for Public-Private Partnership projects, the consent of 70% of landowners is required

- When the government acquires the land for setting up private companies, the consent of 80% of landowners is required

Q3. Discuss social impact assessment study?

Ans: As mentioned under the act, if a real estate company intends to acquire land for public purposes, it requires consulting the panchayats/Municipal Corporations and conducting a social impact assessment study in the affected areas.

Q4. What is included in the social impact assessment study?

Ans: As per the act, the social impact assessment study includes the following:

- evaluation of whether the planned purchase is for the public purpose;

- Estimation of the number of families impacted and the number of families likely to be displaced ;

- the degree to which the proposed acquisition would impact public and private property, buildings, villages, and other common assets;

- whether the proposed acquisition of land is the absolute bare-minimum amount required for the project;

- if land acquisition at a different location has been considered but found out;

- Study of the project's social consequences, the scope and expense of resolving them, and the effect of these costs on the project's total costs.

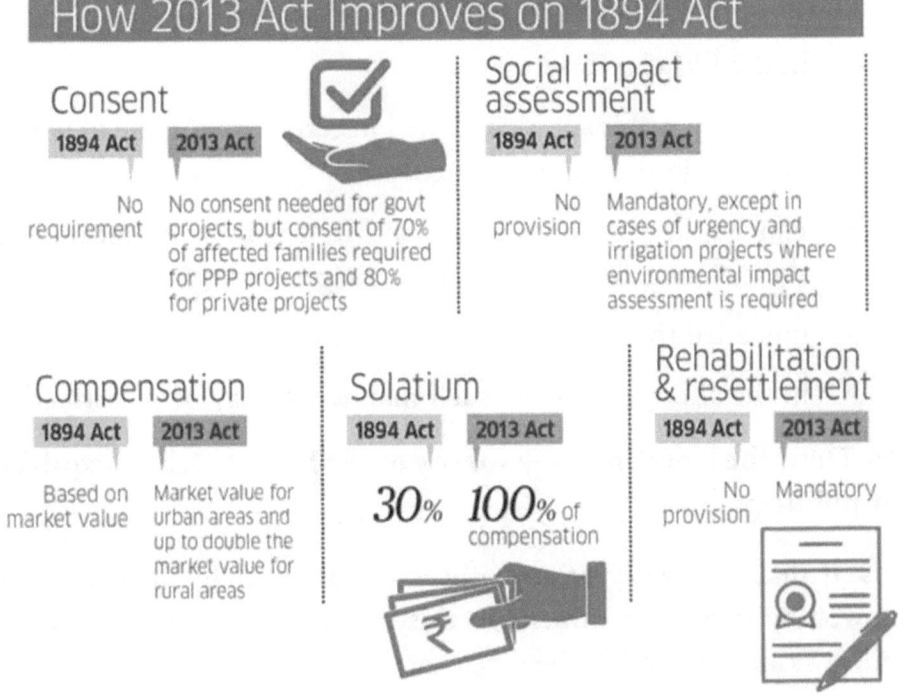

Q5. Is a Public hearing necessary for a social impact assessment study?

Ans: Yes, as mentioned under the act, if a real estate company acquires land for public purpose development, it requires a public hearing and ascertains the views of the affected families.

Q6. Is there some sought of exemption from social impact assessment study?

Ans: Yes, under section 9 of the act, when land is acquired invoking the urgency provision, there can be an exemption of nat taking a social impact assessment study.

Q7. Where the publication of acquiring such lands be published?

Ans: The following are the specifics of the land that will be purchased in rural and urban areas shall be published-

- in the Official Gazette;
- two daily newspapers circulated in certain area's, one of which must be in the regional language;
- Panchayats, Municipalities, or Municipal Corporations, as the case may be, in the local language;
- uploaded to the relevant Government's website;
- in the affected areas, in such manner, as may be prescribed.

Q8. Describe a preliminary survey of the land which is acquired for public purpose?

Ans: It shall be lawful for any officer, either generally or specifically allowed by such Government in this regard, as well as his servants and workmen, to decide the extent of land to be acquired—

- To enter any land in such a place, survey it, and take levels of it. ;
- To excavate the sub-soil;
- To perform all other actions required to determine if the land is suitable for such a purpose;
- To define the limits of the land that will be taken and the planned line of the work that will be done on it; and

- Placemarks and cut trenches to mark certain ranges, borders, and lines where the survey cannot be done otherwise.

Q9. Describe payment for damages mentioned under the act?

Ans: The officer at the time of entry pay for any damage caused, and if in case of dispute as to the sufficiency of the amount so paid, the dispute shall be referred to the decision of the Collector of the district, and such a decision shall be final.

Q10. Describe the Rehabilitation and resettlement scheme is preparation done by the administrator?

Ans: Under section 16 of the Act, after the publication of the primary notification by the collector of such district, the Administrator for Rehabilitation and Resettlement shall conduct a survey and undertake a census of the affected families, which shall include the following things-

- Details of each affected family's land and immovable property acquisitions;
- Land losers and landless people whose livelihoods are largely dependent on the lands being purchased are losing their livelihoods;
- A list of public utilities and Government buildings that are affected or likely to be affected, where resettlement of affected families is involved;
- Details of the infrastructure and services that are likely to be impacted or impacted, in cases where affected families are relocating; and
- Information on any common property properties that are being acquired.

Q11. How the review of the Rehabilitation and resettlement scheme takes place under the act?

Ans: The district's collector has the power to review the Rehabilitation and resettlement scheme submitted by the administrator while he makes the primary scheme as mentioned under the act. After the scheme gets approved by the collector, it shall be made available to the people of such districts in the local language as well.

Q12. Describe the determination of the value of land?

Ans: Under section 26 of the act, the determination of the value of land is described. The collector needs to take the following steps:

- The market value, as specified by the Indian Stamp Act of 1899, for the registration of agreements to sell or sale deeds, as the case may be, in the location where the land is located; or
- The average selling price for a similar form of land in the nearby village or neighbourhood area; or
- In the case of land acquisition for private corporations or public-private partnership programs, the compensation amount is determined under section 2 subsection (2).

Q13. What sought of parameters are to be considered in determining an award?

Ans: The parameters that are to be considered in determining an award are as follows:

- the award sum in compliance with the First and Second Schedules, and the market value as calculated under section 26,
- the loss incurred by the individual involved as a result of the removal of any standing crops and trees on the property at the time of acquisition,

- the damage sustained by the person interested, at the time of acquiring such land,
- The loss incurred by the individual involved at the time of taking possession of the land as a result of the acquisition injuring his other property, movable or immovable, in some way, or his earnings;
- The consequence of the acquisition of the land the person interested is compelled to change his residence or place of business, the reasonable expenses incidental to such change;
- The damage bona fide resulting from diminution of the profits of the land, and
- Any other ground which may be beneficial to the affected families and in the interest of equity and justice.

Q14. Discuss the determination of value and award of solatium?

Ans: The Collector, in deciding the market value of the dwelling and other immovable property or properties attached to the land or building, as well as the value of trees and plants attached to the land or building, land/value of the standing crops damaged during the process of land acquisition, may use the services of experienced persons in the field of agriculture and provide the award of solatium.

Q15. What shall be included in the Rehabilitation and Resettlement Award?

Ans: The following things are to be included in the Rehabilitation and Resettlement Award. The same are as follows:

- Amount due to the family for rehabilitation and relocation.
- number of the person's bank account to which the rehabilitation and resettlement reward money will be transferred.

- details of the house site and the house that will be assigned to displaced families.
- Specifics of the land allocated to displaced families.
- Particulars of one-time subsistence allowance and transportation allowance in case of displaced families & etc.

Q16. Discuss the Reservations as mentioned under the act?

Ans: As mentioned under the act, the benefits, including the reservation benefits available to the Scheduled Tribes and the Scheduled Castes in the affected areas, shall continue in the resettlement area.

Q17. Describe the Apportionment of compensation mentioned under the act?

Ans: When persons are interested in the apportionment of the compensation, the particulars of such apportionment shall be specified in the award, and as between such persons, the award will be definitive proof of the apportionment's correctness. In case of dispute arising as to the apportionment of the amount, the Collector may refer such disputes to the Authority.

Q18. Discuss the penal sections as discussed under the act?

Ans: Section 84-90 of the act deals with the offences and penalties.

The punishment for false information is imprisonment which may extend up to 6 months and a fine up to 1 lakhs or both, and penalties for contravention of the provisions can be extended for up to three years with a fine.

If a company does an offence, then that will be deemed to be guilty of the offence and shall be liable to be proceeded against and punished accordingly.

CHAPTER 8

BENAMI PROPERTY & ENEMY PROPERTY

Benami transactions under the act prohibit certain types of financial transactions. The act defines a Benami transaction as a transaction in which property is transferred to one person for a consideration paid by another person. Such transactions were common in India's economy, typically involving the purchase of real estate, and were thought to contribute to the country's black money problem. The act prohibits all Benami transactions and empowers the government to seize Benami's property and properties without compensation.

The Act establishes four authorities with authority to investigate Benami transactions. They are as follows-

- Initiating officer- Responsible for making notice and attachment of the property.

- Approving Authority- Responsible for giving the notice to provide evidence.

- Administrator- Responsible for taking the possession and management of properties confiscated.

- Adjudicating Authority- Responsible for confiscation and having the vested interest of the property.

Q1. Describe Benami Transactions and Benami Property as mentioned under the Act?

Ans: As discussed under the act, Benami Property refers to such properties as an outcome of a Benami transaction and includes any proceeds from such property.

Benami transaction refers to such transactions wherein property has been transferred to a person without an intention to benefit that person and the consideration of such property is paid by another person.

In the case, Thakur Bhim Singh v. Thakur Kan Singh. It includes two types of Benami transactions:

i. When the person buys the property with his own money but in the name of another person without any intention to benefit another person.

ii. Second case When a property owner completes a conveyance in favour of another without intending to transfer the title to the property, this is known as a Benami transaction. In the following scenario, the transferor remains the true owner.

Q2. Who shall be guilty of the offence committed under Benami Transaction?

Ans: The following people shall be guilty of the offence committed under Benami Transaction Act:

- Beneficial owner
- Benamidar
- Anyone who aids or induces another person to engage in a Benami transaction.

The offences are non-cognizable and non-bailable.

Q3. Whether a particular transaction is Benami in nature?

Ans: In the case of Valliammal v. Subramaniam, the Supreme Court ruled that when determining whether a transaction is Benami in nature, the following six factors should be considered:

1. The funding source of the purchase;

2. After the purchase, the nature and possession of the property;

3. Any motive to give the transaction a Benami connotation;

4. The parties' respective positions and, if any, the claimant's relationship with the accused benamidar;

5. After the sale, who has custody of the title deeds; and

6. The action of the parties involved in the post-sale handling of the land.

According to the Court, the Trial Court and the High Court also erred in transferring the burden of proof to the Defendants to show that the selling transactions were not Benami transactions.

Q4. Discuss Prohibition of Benami Transactions?

Ans: As mentioned under the act, No person shall be involved in any Benami transactions. Suppose any person entering into any such kind of transaction will be punished with imprisonment which can be up to 3 years or fine or both.

Q5. Does the property held Benami liable to confiscation?

Ans: Yes, as mentioned under the act, any property held Benami Property is liable to confiscation. The Central Government does the Confiscation.

Q6. Is Re-transfer of Benami property allowed?

Ans: No, a re-transfer of Benami property is not allowed under the act. If in case any property had been re-transferred, then such transaction will be held null and void.

Q7. Describe the right to recover property that is a Benami property?

Ans: No, the right to recover property that is Benami property is prohibited under the act as mentioned under section 4 of the Act.

Q8. Describe the Adjudicating Authority under the Act?

Ans: The Appellate Tribunal established under the prevention of money laundering act, 2002 discharges the functions of the adjudicating authority and appellate tribunal under the act.

Q9. Discuss the Attachment of the Benami property as mentioned under the Act?

Ans: As mentioned under section 24 of the act, when the Initiating Officer comes to know that a person owns the property which is a Benami property, during the time stated in the notice, the property may be alienated; he may, with the prior approval of the Approving Authority, attach the property provisionally by order in writing, in such manner as may be prescribed, for a period not exceeding to 90 days from the date of issue of notice.

Q10. To whom the notice can be served?

Ans: The notice under section can be served to the following persons. They are as follows:
- Individual;
- To a Company;

- To the Karta of HUF;
- To partnership firms, Joint ventures, etc.

Q11. Describe Confiscation and vesting of Benami Property?

Ans: Where an order is made in respect of any Benami property, the Adjudicating Authority shall, after giving the individual an opportunity to be heard, make an order confiscating the property held to be a Benami property, according to section 27 of the Act.

The rights and title to such assets will be fully vested in the Central Government after issuing a confiscation order.

When no order of confiscation is made then no claim will be against the Govt.

Q12. Discuss such confiscated property management and possession of such properties?

Ans: As mentioned under the act, the Administrator can manage the confiscated properties and take applicable steps to require care of such properties as directed by the Central Government.

Post which the Appropriate Authority shall serve the notice the persons involved with the Benami property which has been confiscated. Such notice must be sent within 7 days.

Q13. Discuss the Appellate Tribunal as mentioned under the Act?

Ans: The Appellate Tribunal established under section 25 of the PML Act may discharge the Adjudicating Authority and Appellate Tribunal functions under the Benami Act.

The power that is vested with Appellate Tribunal has certain vested power. The power is as follows:

- May summon and compel the presence of any person, as well as examine him under oath.
- To determine a case where sufficient evidence is present;
- Has the power to admit additional evidence which was previously not admitted by the appropriate authority.
- Has the power to call upon any witness or any document which it feels to be the part of such proceedings
- Can pass upon certain orders as it deems fit for meeting the ends of the justice.
- Can review its decisions.

Q14. Who has the power to transfer the case?

Ans: The Chairperson of the Appellate Tribunal has the power to transfer the case, and if the case was pending before one Bench, it could transfer to any other Bench. On the application of any parties and after hearing them.

Q15. Can an appeal be filed in the High Court?

Ans: As mentioned under the act, the aggrieved party can file an appeal in the high court as mentioned under section 49 of the act within 60 days.

Q16. Discuss the offences and penalties under the act?

Ans: Under the act, the penalty for Benami Transactions is rigorous imprisonment, which may extend up to 7 years and a fine that stands at 25% of the property's market value.

The penalty for providing any false information about such transactions is Imprisonment, which may extend up to 5 years and a fine that stands at 10% of the property's market value.

Certain provisions deal with offences made by the companies. It says that if offences did by the companies, then such company shall be guilty of contravention of such sections and shall be liable to be punished accordingly.

ENEMY PROPERTY ACT

Enemy properties are properties that an enemy individual or enemy company holds. The individuals mentioned are no longer the citizens of a particular country wherein they are deemed to be Enemies.

The concept of Enemy Property came into the picture back in the 1960s where India was at war with China and Pakistan. The properties were confiscated by the Central Govt. under the Defense Act of India.

The enemy was mentioned under the act, which includes a person or the firm, an enemy under the Defense of India Act, 1962.

Q1. What do you mean by the term Enemy?

Ans: The term enemy defines any country and residents of that country performed external belligerence against India. The word "Enemy Subject" and "Enemy Firm" are described in the Act to include an enemy's legal heir and successor, whether a citizen of India or a citizen of a country that is not an enemy; and an enemy's succeeding firm, regardless of the nationality of its members or partners.

> The properties included land, buildings, shares held in companies, gold and jewellery of the citizens of enemy countries.
>
> The responsibility of the administration of enemy properties was handed over to the Custodian of Enemy Property (an office under GOI).
>
> The Defense of India Acts were temporary laws that ceased to operate after the wars ended.
>
> To administer the enemy property seized during the wars, the government enacted the Enemy Property Act in 1968.

Q2. Define Enemy Property?

Ans: An Enemy Property means that any property for time is held, managed on behalf of the enemy, subject to enemy property. Property those interests are vested in the Central Govt. as they are the custodian of such properties.

Q3. How is an enemy property dealt with in India?

Ans: The Enemy Property Act of 1968 mandated that enemy property be continuously vested in the Custodian of Enemy Property for India. In the Central Government, the Custodian controls enemy assets distributed through several states in the country.

Q4. Discuss the custodian of enemy property for India & deputy custodian?

Ans: The Central Government is responsible for enforcing the Act's provisions appoints the enemy property custodian for India and one or more Deputy Custodians and Assistant Custodians.

Q5. Describe the Issue Certificate by custodian?

Ans: The Custodian may declare that the property of the enemy, the enemy subject, or the enemy firm mentioned in the order vests in him under this Act and issue a certificate to that effect, and such certificate shall be the proof of the truth, after making such inquiries as he deems appropriate.

Q6. Describe the prohibition to transfer any property vested in Custodian by an enemy?

Ans: The act prohibits all transfers by an enemy of enemy property. The enemy has no right to transfer that property which is considered to be enemy property.

Q7. Discuss the power of the custodian?

Ans: As per section 8 of the Act, The following are the power of the custodian:

- Carry on the enemy's business,
- Take steps to reclaim any funds owed to the enemy,
- Make any contract and execute any document in the enemy's name and on his behalf.,
- Any suit or other legal action should be instituted, defended, or continued,
- raise any loans that may be required on the property's protection,
- Any of the properties can be sold, mortgaged, leased, or otherwise disposed of,
- make payments to the enemy and his dependents& Etc.

Q8. Can the Custodian sell the enemy property?

Ans: Yes, as mentioned under the act, the enemy property is sold by the Custodian as mentioned under section 8A.

Q9. Describe the legal action taken against businesses whose properties have been entrusted to the Custodian?

Ans: As discussed under the act under section 14, where the enemy property vested in the Custodian under this Act consists of assets of the company, no proceeding, civil or criminal, shall be instituted under the Companies Act except with the consent in writing of the Custodian.

Q10. Discuss the offences and penalties under the act?

Ans: When any person makes any payment in contravention to the custodian of money, payable to an enemy, enemy subject, or enemy firm, such payment shall be void and liable to punish with imprisonment for a term extending to six months or with a fine or both.

When any person contravenes the transfer of securities belongings to an enemy shall be liable for imprisonment for extends to six months or with a fine or with both.

When any person fails to comply with the custodian's powers to summon persons and call for documents, they shall be punished by a fine of up to five hundred rupees.

If any person fails to submit the return as to enemy property or furnishes such return which knows to be false or does not believe to be true, he shall be subject to a fine of up to five hundred rupees.

CHAPTER 9

THE COMPETITION ACT, 2002

The Competition Act, 2002 was established to administer the competition in the Indian Market. It was replaced by the Monopolies and Restrictive Trade Practices Act, 1969. Under the Act, the Competition Commission of India was established to prevent activities that harm competition in India. It is a tool to implement and enforce competition policy and prevent and punish anti-competitive business practices by firms and unnecessary Government interference. Competition laws are equally applicable on written and oral agreements, arrangements between the enterprises or persons.

Broadly, the Commission's duty is:-

To prohibit the agreements or practices that have or are likely to have an appreciable adverse effect on competition in a market in India (horizontal and vertical agreements/conduct);

To prohibit the abuse of dominance in a market;

To prohibit acquisitions, mergers, amalgamations, etc., between enterprises that have or are likely to have an appreciable adverse effect on competition in the market in India.

Why MRTP Failed?

MRTP Act, 1969 has become obsolete in certain areas in the light of international economic developments relating to competition laws. So, the need was felt to shift the focus from curbing monopolies to promoting competition. Hence, the Competition Act, 2002 was enacted to remove the rigidly structured MRTP Act, 1969.

The Competition Act, 2002 is flexible, behaviour oriented and explicitly indicates the parameters that shall be kept in view while deciding the adverse effect on competition, abuse of dominance, and prejudicial combinations. The main purpose of the Act is to ensure free and fair competition in the market.

Key differences between MRTP Act and Competition Act:

- MRTP Act is based on the pre-liberalization scenario, whereas Competition Act is based on the post-liberalization scenario.
- MRTP Act emphasizes curbing monopolies, whereas Competition Act emphasizes promoting competition.
- MRTP Act provides for compulsory registration of agreements relating to restrictive trade practices, whereas in the Competition Act, there is no such requirement of registration of agreements.
- Under Competition Act, dominance per se is not bad, but only the abuse of dominance is considered bad, whereas dominance itself is bad under the MRTP Act.
- MRTP Act does not regulate combinations, whereas Competition Act regulates them.
- MRTP Act does not vest MRTP Commission power to inquire into cartels of foreign origin in a direct manner, whereas the Competition Act seeks to regulate them.

Q1. Impact of DLF Case in the Real Estate Sector?

Ans: The Competition Commission of India (CCI), the regulator under the act, in Belaire Owners' Association v DLF Limited and HUDA, imposed a penalty of ₹6.3 billion (US$115 million) on the real estate giant DLF for abuse of dominant position through unfair conditions in its contracts with flat buyers and directed

DLF to "cease and desist" from framing and imposing such unfair conditions and to modify them within three months. The penalty imposed on DLF has been calculated as 7% of its average group turnover for the past three fiscal years and is the heaviest penalty imposed by the CCI to date. The CCI, by this order, advised the central and state governments to draft stringent and deterrent laws for the real estate sector.

This order is expected to have vast repercussions in the real estate domain, which has been buffeted by high inflation and hefty home loan rates. Project delays are often beyond the developers' control and stringent conditions imposed by the CCI, or the courts could seriously harm the real estate sector.

This order is noteworthy because:-

1. it is the first time that competition law has targeted the manipulative nature of "abuse of dominant position";

2. it overtakes the well-known concept of "unfair trade practices", usually applied in cases of consumer disputes;

3. it brings to the fore the wrongful practices of builders that receive the money from buyers for one project and then siphon it away for other projects; and

4. it shows that CCI decisions follow US and EU case precedents while the methodology adopted to calculate hefty penalties lacks foundation in the specific provisions of the act.

Q2. What are Anti-Competitive Agreements?

Ans: As per the Act, under Section 3 which prevents any enterprise or association from entering into any agreement which causes or is likely to cause an appreciable adverse effect on competition (AAEC) within India.

Case laws:

The United States v. Misle Bus & Equipment Co, it was held that bid rigging is per se illegal irrespective of the fact that it does not matter whether the agreement concerns the low bid, the quantum of the individual bidders bidding and the bidder who would win the contract.

THE CEMENT CARTEL CASE:

In 2011 Indian Builders Association filed a complaint with CCI against 10 cement manufacturers and their trade associations alleging cartelisation, price-fixing and limiting production and supply. The CCI issues an order stating that the activity of the cement companies is guilty of anti-competitive practices like collusive price, parallelism in supply and dispatch, creating artificial scarcity by limiting output to raise prices etc.

Q3. What is an appreciable adverse effect on the competition?

Ans: Appreciable Adverse effects on competition refer to various economic factors, some of which have been laid out under section 19 of the Act, such as "creation of barriers of new entrants in the market, driving existing competitors out, accrual of consumer benefits, etc.

Q4. Discuss the case of *Builders Association of India vs Cement manufactures association*?

Ans: In Builders Association of India v. Cement Manufacturers' Association, the CCI held some of the cement manufacturers guilty of violating sections 3(3)(a) and (b) of the Act. The presumption of anti-competitive agreements can be inferred from the intention or conduct of parties and can be established by circumstantial evidence alone. Thus, it was held that the circumstantial evidence of parallel changes in the prices and production of goods along with 'plus factors' indicated that the cement companies had formed a cartel to

a. directly or indirectly determine purchase or sale prices and

b. limit or control production, supply, markets, technical development, investment, or provision of services

Moreover, that there was no requirement of an explicit agreement to prove the same. Factors such as sharing of information amongst the 11 cement manufacturers that could facilitate price-fixing and identical prices, manufacturing units, and dispatch rates after certain meetings were the "plus factors" that supported the presumption of cartelization. Cement companies were accused of meeting regularly to fix prices, control market share, and hold back supply, leading to market dominance and gaining illegal profits. CCI had imposed a fine of Rs. 63.07 billion on 11 cement companies for the cartel.

Q5. How bid-rigging impacts the real-estate industry?

Ans: Bid rigging means any agreement between organisations or persons wherein they are engaged in identical or similar production or trading of goods or provision of services, which has the effect of eliminating or reducing competition for bids or adversely affecting or manipulating the process for bidding as discussed under section 3 of the Act.

Western Coalfields Limited v. SSV Coal Carriers Pvt Ltd.: The CCI has imposed a cumulative penalty of Rs. 120 Million on ten coal and sand transporters for bid-rigging. The OPs were found to have rigged the bids submitted in relation to fourth tenders for coal and sand transportation floaters by Western Coalfields Limited, a subsidiary of the state-owned monopolist, Coal India Ltd.

Q6. Describe Dominant position under the act?

Ans: Dominant Position has been defined as a position enjoyed by an enterprise whereby enables it to operate independently of competitive forces prevailing in the relevant market or affect its competitors or consumers or the relevant market in its favour.

Q7. Describe the Abuse of Dominant position by the enterprises present in the market?

Ans: An enterprise in a dominant position performs any such act that gives rise to the abuse of the position which the enterprises hold in the market. Some of the following acts are as follows-

Directly or indirectly, imposes unfair or discriminatory practices;

Limits or restricts the production of goods or provision of any services in any form;

Indulges in practice or practices resulting in a denial of market access;

Concludes contracts subject to acceptance by other parties of supplementary obligations which have no connection with the subject of such contracts;

Uses its dominant position in one relevant market to enter into another relevant market.

Case: In the case of Shri Neeraj Malhotra v. North Delhi Power Ltd 11th May 2011, the Competition Commission of India held that according to Section 4 of the Competition Act of India, a prohibition towards the nature of holding a dominant position is not issued to any organization, but a strict and special responsibility on such organizations is issued, requiring them to not to abuse their dominant position. Having noted that, the CCI fails to enlist and observe the various activities which are prohibited under this section. What amounts to abuse of dominance is a subjective matter and shall depend on case-to-case basis, taking into consideration the circumstances and situations of each case.

Q8. Describe predatory pricing, which is mentioned under the Act?

Ans: Predatory pricing is a strategy where a company that has a dominant position in the market lower its price so that other companies would be bound to get out of the market as they cannot sell those products at such low rates.

Q9. Discuss Combinations under the competition Act?

Ans: As per Competition Act, combination is the merger between two or more enterprises or firms or the business sector acquisitions (such as companies or firms) by other business enterprises. The Government has control over combinations, mergers and acquisitions within the country to promote competition and thereby to keep in check those small-scale establishments are not overshadowed and swallowed by more reputed industries. This is because the merger of big shot companies reduces competition and makes it difficult and almost impossible for smaller firms to grow or profit from their business. The accumulation of wealth in certain sectors of business and consumer concerns can lead to major economic and social discrepancies within the nation.

Case Law: Role of Competition Law in National Interest vis-à-vis Public Interest

The two companies involved in this case the Tata Oil Mills company limited (TOMCO) and Hindustan lever Limited (HLL), which is a subsidiary of Uni-Lever (UL), a multinational company. Both the companies when manufacturers of soaps, detergents, toiletries and animal feeds. As TOMCO voice incoming losses from 1990 to 1991, its board of directors decided to amalgamate their company with HLL, which happened to be a more prosperous and successful company in the same field of activities and the proposal was even accepted by HLL. The board of directors of both the companies a large majority of shareholders, debenture holders and others accepted the scheme of amalgamation.

However, two of the shareholders of TOMCO, irregularities of provisions of the Companies Act, MRTP Act, preferential allotment of shares to Uni-lever, on less than the market value the high court held that HLL was already the holder of 51% shares before any allotment. Hence, the allotment at a lower price placed them at par with the same holding was neither illegal nor violates public interest. The matter was referred to the Supreme Court.

Decision and Reasons:

The Supreme Court judges delivered two separate but concurrent judgement. Dealing more elaborately with the question of public interest, Justice Sen stated that merely because 51 % of shares of HLL specifically to encourage foreign participation of businesses in India.

Q10. Can the Competition Commission of India pass the order to know about the abuse of the dominant position?

Ans: Yes. According to section 27 of the act, the commission can pass orders when it feels that an organisation has abused its dominant position in the market. The following things can be passed by the commission through orders wherein the enterprise has violated the provisions under the act-

Direct such enterprise to discontinue such agreements

Impose penalty as it finds fit but not more than 10% of the average of turnover of last 3 years

Direct the enterprise to modify such changes

Direct the enterprise for abiding by the orders passed by the Commission etc.

Q11. What are the penalties for contraventions of orders passed by the commission?

Ans: The penalties for contraventions of orders passed by the commission are imprisonment for a term which might extend up to 3 years and a fine which might extend up to 25 crores as per section 42 of the Act.

Q12. What are the penalties for non-furnishing of information on combinations?

Ans: The penalties for non-furnishing of information on Combinations as per section 43 A of the act states that the commission shall impose penalties on such enterprises, extending to one percent of the total turnover or the assets, whichever is higher.

Q13. What are the penalties for making false statement or omission to furnish material information?

Ans: The penalty for making a false statement or omission to furnish material information as per the act is a penalty that is not less than 50 lakhs and should not exceed 1 Crore.

Q14. Discuss the contravention made by companies?

Ans: As discussed under the act, under section 48, it defines both company and director. It also says that the company shall be guilty of the contraventions made as mentioned under the act shall be liable and punished accordingly.

Taking everything into account, I might want to add that the cement organizations are attempting to climb the costs of cement bags. However, this is because the Covid-19 demand destruction has postponed new capacity additions and the possibility of a diminished demand-supply gap. The Indian cement industry has been home to more supply capacity than demand. Before the pandemic, the industry's demand-supply mismatch was expected to narrow in FY21 and the years ahead. For the cement price hike seen so far in May, the southern markets in India saw the highest rise. The average price for Rs. 50/cement bag.

CHAPTER 10

THE TRANSFER OF PROPERTY ACT, 1882

Background and history of transfer of property act

The Transfer of Property Act, 1882 came into force on the first day of July 1882. The act is not and does not purport to be an exhaustive enactment. Section 5 of the Transfer of Property Act defines 'Transfer of Property. It means an act by which a living person conveys property in present or future to one or more living persons, himself, or himself, and one or more other living persons. A living person includes a Company, Association, or body of individuals. The Transfer of Property Act deals with the sale, mortgage, gift, lease, and exchange. Hence, abandonment is not a transfer. Partition is not a transfer. Transfer to himself and others: This is possible in the case of trust. Future property can be transferred (subject to Section 6.). The persons must be competent to make a contract. Registration, under the Registration Act, is compulsory if the value of the immovable property is worth Rs.100/- and above.

Q1. What is meant by Attestation? What are the requisites of a valid attestation? Point out the legal effect of attestation.

Ans: The T.P. Act defines attestation in Section 3. Attesting in respect of an instrument means that,

    a. the documents must be attested by two or more witnesses, each of whom has seen the executants sign or affix his mark to the document.

b. each of them must have signed the instrument in the presence of the executant.

c. The attestors must have animus attest and (intention of attesting).

d. It is not necessary that more than one should be present at the same time.

e. Law also does not prescribe any particular form of attestation.

f. The usual procedure is that the attestors must sign with the address and date.

The Privy Council in Shamu vs Abdul Khandir resolved the controversy of whether the attestors should have seen the execution or not of the document. It held that the attestors who sign the document must have seen the document executed. This was accepted in Section 3, but it is given retrospective effect. In English law, attestors should all be present simultaneously and must have seen the execution. However, it is not so, according to Indian Law. Attestors should be sui juris (person legally capable). Even thumb impression is allowed. Attestation does not mean that attestors have notice of the contents of the document. However, attestation stops from denying the factum of execution. They vouch to the execution, not to contents.

Q2. What is immovable property?

Ans: TPA deals with various transfers with respect to immovable property. Section 3(2) says, Immovable Property does not include standing timber, growing crops, or grass. The General Classes Act says Immovable Property includes lands, benefits that arise out of the land, and things attached to the earth. 'Attached to the earth' means rooted to the earth, i.e., trees, shrubs, etc., embedded in the earth, i.e., walls or buildings, attached to what is so embedded. Further right to receive future rent is Immovable Property. Marshall v. Green: Sale of trees to be cut and taken away. Held: the sale was not for

Immovable Property. If the parties intend that the trees should have further nutriment from the land, then it is Immovable Property otherwise not. In English Law, there is the doctrine of fixtures. Whether a chattel is resetting merely by its weight on the floor, it is not immovable. In Holland V. Hodgson: a mortgage of a mill was made. Held: The mortgage also covered certain looms attached to the stone of the mill.

Q3. What is specs succession?

Ans: It means 'Chance of Succession'.

Section 6 of Transfer of Property Act provides that the chance of an heir succeeding to an estate or a relation obtaining a legacy of a Kinsman or such a mere possibility cannot be transferred. E.g.: The interest of a reversionary on the death of a Hindu widow. In Amrit Narayana Vs. Gaya Singh: 'A' hoping to succeed to the property of his maternal grandfather B, sold to C, his such interest, during the lifetime of B. Subsequently B died. A sued for recovery of property from C. Held: The sale was of succession and therefore void. Future interests in properties such as contingent interest or executory interest are transferable, as, here, the possibility is coupled with an interest. Similar to spes successions, the possibilities of a like nature are:

i. Chance of a person deriving income from scavenging work, which he expects to get in the future.

ii. Right of a priest to share in the offerings at the temple. There is a mere chance and hence inalienable.

Q4. What is the charge on a property under the transfer of property act?

Ans: Where immovable property of a {person is by an act of parties, (or by operation of law) made security |or the payment of money to another, the latter person is said to have a charge on the property.

Conditions:

i. The transaction should not amount to a mortgage.

ii. All matters relating to the rights and liabilities of the parties to the charge are governed by those applicable to a simple mortgage. (Section 59).

iii. This will not apply to a trustee^ who makes a charge on the trust property.

iv. Bona fide transferees without notice of the charge on the immovable property are protected. A charge is an encumbrance on the property.

v. The formalities to be observed to create a charge are the same as for a simple mortgage. There is no transfer of any interest in the immovable property in a charge, as in a mortgage.

There is the creation of a right of payment out of the property specified. A charge is less than a simple mortgage & cannot take priority over it. A charge cannot bind a bona fide purchaser for value who had no notice of the charge.

Q5. What is an exception under the Transfer of Property Act?

Ans: Section 6 of the Transfer of Property Act provides exceptions to the rule that property of any kind may be transferred. The exceptions are:

a. Spes Successions.

b. Transfer of Right of Re-entry and Easement.

c. Religious Office.

d. Serving of Inams.

e. Maintenance Right.

f. Mere right to sue.

g. Public Office, stipends and pensions,

h. Illegal transfers.

Q6. What is a "gift" and a gift of immovable property that can be affected? When can a gift be suspended or revoked?

Ans: Section 122 of TPA defines the term gift. 'It is the transfer of certain existing movable or immovable property made voluntarily and without consideration and accepted by or on behalf of the donee'. The person who makes the gift is the donor.

The donee must accept the gift:

a. during the donor's lifetime and

b. While the donor is still capable of giving the property gifted. But if the donee dies before acceptance, the gift is void.

Gift of movable property may be registered or may be affected by delivery. However, the gift of immovable property of any value requires registration under section 17 (a) of the Registration Act. It must be signed by the donor and must be attested by two witnesses. The property must be existing at the time of the gift. A gift of future property is void. When a gift is made to several persons and one or more donees does not accept, it is void of respect for those who do not accept it.

Q7. Define lease. Distinguish between lease and license.

Ans: Section 105 of the Transfer of Property Act defines a lease. A lease of immovable property is defined as the transfer of the right to enjoy such property made for a particular amount of time, considering a price paid or promised. The consideration may be a fixed amount or a share of crops or serving of any other thing to be rendered periodically or otherwise. A lease may be oral or in writing.

If the lease is for one year or above, it must be in writing and registered. Lease for the lesser period may be oral or in writing. Registration is optional. Delivery of possession is necessary for both circumstances.

➤ DISTINCTION BETWEEN LEASE AND LICENCE:

1. A lease is a transfer of an interest in a specific immovable property, while a license is a bare permission without any transfer of an interest.

2. A lease creates an interest favouring the lessee concerning the property, but a license does not create such an interest.

3. A lease is the tenant can create both transferable and heritable, a sub-tenancy and on the death of the tenant, the tenancy can be inherited by his/her legal heir, whereas a license is neither transferable nor heritable

4. A license comes to an end with the death of either the grantor or the guarantee since it is a personal contract, but a lease does not come to an end on either the death of the grantor or grantee.

5. A license can be withdrawn at any time at the pleasure of the grantor, but the lease can come to an end only following the terms and conditions stipulated in the contract of a tenancy agreement.

6. A lease is unaffected by the transfer of the property by sale favouring a third party. It continues and the purchaser has to wait till the time for which the tenancy was created is over before he can get the possession, whereas, in the case of a license, if the property is sold to a third party, it comes to an end immediately.

7. A lessee has a right to protect the possession in his own right. Whereas a licensee cannot defend his possession in his name as he does not have any proprietary right in the property.

8. A lessee in possession of the property is entitled to any improvements or accessions made to the property, while a licensee is not.

Q8. What are the rights and liabilities of a lessor and a lessee?

Ans: RIGHTS AND DUTIES OF THE LESSOR AND LESSEE

As per section 108 of the Transfer of Property Act, the rights and liabilities of the lessor and lessee are as follows:

The rights and liabilities of the lessor are as follows:

a. The lessor should disclose any material or latent defects in the property leased.

b. The lessor must put the lessee in possession of the property.

c. There is a covenant for quite an enjoyment of the property if the lessee pays the rent during the lease period.

The rights and liabilities of the lessee are as follows:

a. Lessee's right to accretions if there is any accretion to the benefit of the property. The lessee is entitled to such accretions. This is of course, subject to the law relating to allusion. Hence adjoining wasteland brought under cultivation is not accretion.

b. Voidable lease: If the material part of the leased property is destroyed (partially or completely) by fire, tempest or floods or violence or by the enemy, the lease is voidable in the opinion of the lessee. Of course, the lessee should not be the cause of the destruction of the property.

c. Right to Sub-lease: Unless prohibited by the lessor under the lease deed, the lessee is entitled to sub-lease.

d. Right to fixtures: Anything affixed to the land becomes part of the land. The lessee is entitled to such fixtures.

e. Right to repairs: Lessee may, by giving reasonable notice to the lessor, make the repairs if the lessor has neglected it. The lessee may deduct such expenses from the rent or he may recover from the lessor.

f. Payment on behalf of the lessor: If the lessor has neglected to make payments (House tax etc.), the lessee has a right to pay and get it reimbursed from the lessor.

g. Right to ingress: The lessee has free ingress (Right to enter) & Egress & to carry any crops grown by the lessee when the lease is terminated.

h. Duty to restore possession: The lessee is bound to restore the property to the lessor in good condition, i.e., as the property was at the time of the lease (subject to the normal wear and tear). However, if the lessee causes the defect, he should not use the property for a purpose different from a purpose agreed upon. He should not fell timber, pull-down or damage buildings, or commit any other destructive or injurious acts thereto.

i. The lessee is bound to pay the rent as agreed upon.

Q9. Explain the rule against perpetuity. What are the exceptions to the rule against perpetuity?

Ans: The rule against perpetuities was announced in Whitby Vs. Mitchell. This has been suitably changed and the rule is laid down in Section. 14 of the Transfer of Property Act. The transfer of property is void if it creates an interest which is to take effect after the lifetime of one or more persons living at the date of such transfer and the minority of some person who shall be in existence at the expiration of that period, and to whom, if he attains full age, the interest created, is to belong. The leading case is Cadell Vs. Palmer: A trust was created for a term of 120 years if 28 named persons or any of them should so long live and from the determination of that term for a further period of 21 years, and after the end of both terms, for the benefit of persons to be then ascertained. The House of Lords held that the transfer was valid in respect of the persons in being and 21 years thereafter.

Q10. What is CONDITION PRECEDENT?

Ans: CONDITION PRECEDENT is one where a valid condition is imposed and the property becomes vested on the fulfilment of the condition thereof. Here the rule of Cypres is applied, i.e., there must be substantial compliance with the condition imposed. The leading case is Edwards Vs. Hammand.

Q11. What is CONDITION SUBSEQUENT?

Ans: A condition subsequent is one where a disposition of property effects only when the condition is fulfilled subsequently. Here the condition should be strictly fulfilled.

Q12. DOCTRINE OF ELECTION. (SECTION.35)

Ans: The doctrine of election was enunciated by the House of Lords in the leading case Cooper Vs. Cooper. It states that there is an obligation on him who takes a benefit under a will or other instrument to give full effect to that instrument under which he takes a benefit. If the transferor has transferred something beyond his power but to which effect could be given by the transferee's consent, the law provides that the person who takes the benefit must also take the obligations thereof. This principle is embodied in Section.35 of the Act.

Q13. BONA FIDE HOLDER & FRAUDULENT TRANSFER

Ans: IMPROVEMENTS MADE BY BONAFIDE HOLDERS UNDER DEFECTIVETITLE. (SECTION 51) DOCTRINE OF ACQUIESCENCE. A transferee of immovable property, believing in good faith that he is entitled thereto, may make improvements on the property. However, if he is subsequently evicted by a person who has a better title, then the transferee has a right to the value of the improvements estimated and paid. He may get this value secured or realized by getting the property sold by the owner to the transferee.

FRAUDULENT TRANSFER (SECTION 53).

Every transfer of immovable property made with intent to defeat or delay the transferor's creditors shall be voidable in the opinion of any creditor so defeated or delayed.

Exceptions:

i. This will not affect the rights of the bona fide transferee for consideration.

ii. This shall not affect insolvency law.

Q14. Discuss the doctrine of 'Lis-Pendens.'

Ans: DOCTRINE OF LIS PENDENS' (SECTION 52) The Doctrine of 'Lis Pendens' has its origin in Bellamy Vs. Sabine. It means pendente lite (pending litigation) neither party to the litigation can transfer the property in dispute so as to affect the interests of his opponent.

The essentials are as follows:

a. The transfer should take place during the pendency of a suit or proceeding.

b. The case must be pending in a court of competent jurisdiction.

c. The case should not be collusive.

d. The litigation should be specified in respect of the immovable property transferred. It is evident from the above that the doctrine does not prohibit transfer 'pendente lite', but what it says is that the transfer should not defeat the other party's rights & any decree which the court may pass.

Q15. Explain DOCTRINE OF PART PERFORMANCE and its nature

Ans: The doctrine originated in England and the leading case in Maddison V. Anderson. The Statute of Frauds required that all contracts relating to land must be in writing. This led to many difficulties.

THE DOCTRINE -When a person contracts to transfer any immovable property by writing signed by him using such terms necessary to constitute a transfer with reasonable certainty, and the transferee has performed or is willing to perform his part of the Contract.

Essentials:

i. The transfer is for valuable consideration. Hence, gifts are excluded.

ii. Writing: There must be a written agreement. Hence, an Oral agreement will not suffice.

iii. The agreement should be signed by the transferor or by his duly authorized agent.

iv. Applies to immovable only.

v. The terms of the Contracts must be capable of being ascertained with reasonable certainty.

vi. The transferee must have immovable property.

vii. The transferee must be ready and willing to perform his part of the Contract.

Q16. Discuss the concept of a contract to sale under the purview of the transfer of property act. What are the rights and duties of seller and buyer?

Ans: Contract of sale (Section.54 T.P Act) is a transfer of ownership in exchange for a price paid or promised or part-paid and part promised. A registered deed can sell the immovable property if the value is Rs.100/- or above. Delivery of the property takes place when the buyer is placed in possession of the property. Contract for sale is an agreement to sell. It is a Contract for the sale of the immovable property on terms settled by parties. This by itself will not create any charge or interest in the property.

Purchase of new flat - Section 53A of Transfer of Property Act, 1882.

Assessee sold a building on 30-4-2004 and claimed deduction under section 54 in respect of capital gain arising on sale of building as he has invested in a new flat on 25-6-2003. i.e. with in one year from date of transfer of building. Assessing Officer was of the view that as registration of transfer deed of building was dated 26-8-2004 hence, claim under section 54 was denied. The Tribunal held that buyer had performed their part of their obligation as on 30-4-2004, in such a situation, mere non registration of transfer deed would not change date of transfer of building to 26-8-2004. Tribunal held that assessee was entitled to deduction under section 54. (A. Y. 2005-06).

- *Sureshchandra Agarwal v. ITO (2011) 48 SOT 210 (Mum.)(Trib.)*

Duties of a seller:

i. The seller is bound to disclose any material defect in the property to the buyer, which the seller is aware of and which cannot be discovered with ordinary care by the buyer (caveat emptor). Otherwise, it becomes fraudulent.

ii. To show the buyer all related documents of title relating to the property.

iii. To answer all relevant questions relating to the title etc., of the property.

iv. To execute a sale deed when the buyer renders the price.

v. To take care of the property from the date of the agreement until the date of the sale.

vi. To give buyer the possession of the property.

vii. To pay all public charges and rents due up to the date of the sale: he should also discharge encumbrances if any, unless the sale is made subject to any encumbrances.

viii. There is a warranty that the seller has the power to transfer and professes that interest he is transferring.

ix. When the sale price is fully paid up, the seller is bound to deliver all the title documents to the buyer.

Rights of a seller:

i. He is entitled to all the rents and profits of the property till the ownership passes to the buyer.

ii. Vendor's lien: when the buyer has become the owner when the sale price has not been fully paid, then the buyer, the Vendor, gets charge over the property for unpaid amounts.

> **Rights and Duties of the buyer:**

Buyer's duties:

The buyer is bound:

i. to disclose to the seller any fact that would materially enhance the property's value; otherwise, it becomes fraudulent.

ii. To pay or tender the price at the time and place to complete the sale. He may adjust pre-paid or earnest money if any.

iii. Where the property has passed to the buyer, the buyer becomes liable for any loss or destruction to the property. Further, as between the seller & buyer, the buyer should pay public charges and rents which may become payable. Rights of the buyer

iv. The buyer is entitled to any benefit and increase in the value, rents etc after the property has passed on to him.

v. The buyer has a charge on the advances made in anticipation of the delivery and for interest in such advances.

Q17. What are the essentials of a Mortgage? Discuss different kinds of Mortgage.

Ans: Definitions and kinds

According to section 58 of the T.P. Act, a mortgage is the transfer of an interest in specific immovable property for the purpose of securing the payment of money advanced. The money may be advanced by way of loan (existing or future) or performance of an act giving rise to a pecuniary liability. The transferor is called the mortgagor, and the transferee the mortgagee.

If the mortgage is made under an instrument, it is called a mortgage deed. The amount secured is the mortgage money. The deed must be registered if the value is Rs. 100 and above. It must be in writing, signed and duly attested.

There are different kinds of mortgages recognised by the T.P. Act:

i. Simple mortgage,

ii. Mortgage by conditional sale,

iii. Usufructuary mortgage,

iv. English mortgage

v. Equitable mortgage (mortgage by deposit of title deeds)

vi. Anomalous mortgage.

Q18. Explain "Once a Mortgage always a Mortgage" with special reference to doctrine on equity of redemption. Illustrate your answer.

Ans: 'Once a Mortgage always a Mortgage or Doctrine of equity of Redemption.Section-60Mortgagor has a right to redeem the mortgage. The court's guard this right called the Equity of redemption. Any contract entered into between the mortgagor and mortgagee imposing condition against this right to redeem cannot be enforced. The right to redeem is part of the transaction. A mortgage is the only security for repayment of debt. Hence, when the debt is paid, the mortgagor is entitled and the mortgagee should release the property thereof. Any condition against this right to redeem is called a 'clog on the equity of redemption.

Q19. Explain the doctrine of Subrogation (Section 91)

Ans: Subrogation means 'Substitution'. This enables a person to pay off a creditor, get into his shoes, and exercise the creditor's rights. Any person redeeming a mortgaged property has the same rights (of redemption, foreclosure or sale) as the mortgagee may have against the mortgagor or any other mortgagee. This right is subrogation. There must be full redemption to apply this doctrine.

Q20. Rights and Liabilities of Mortgagee in possession.

Ans: Rights of the mortgagee:

i. The mortgagee may spend any necessary amount for

   a. The preservation of the mortgaged property from destruction, forfeiture, or sale.

   b. for supporting the mortgagor's title.

   c. to make his title good against the mortgagor (defending suits against mortgagor).

ii. Where the mortgaged property is sold under Revenue sales or acquired by Govt., the mortgagee is entitled to claim his money the surplus of proceeds of such sale or acquisition.

Liabilities of the mortgagee:

i. Mortgagee should prudently manage the property.

ii. He must make endeavours to collect the rents & profits.

iii. He must pay all Govt. revenues & Public charges and all rents due. (This is subject to agreement)

iv. Necessary repairs to the property are to be made from a collection of rent etc.

v. He should not do anything to destroy or damage the property.

vi. He must maintain clear, full, and accurate accounts.

vii. When the mortgagor tenders or deposits any money, the mortgagee should account for the same.

Q21. Discuss Substituted Security: Section.73

Ans: Section. 73 of the TOPA Act deals with Substituted security, with reference to a mortgage. This means the mortgagee for his security is entitled to the subject-of mortgage property and anything that may be substituted for it. Hence, if the mortgaged property takes a new form, the security extends to that also.

Q22. Doctrine of Consolidation (Section 61 & 67A)

Ans: This has its origin in the English concept of the "Equity of consolidation" and with some modification, it is incorporated in our T.P. Act. When a mortgagor executes two or more mortgages favouring the same mortgagee, and when the mortgage money of two or more becomes due, the mortgagor may redeem each mortgage separately or consolidate two or more of such mortgages together. This applies to cases of two (or more) mortgages by the same mortgagor to the same or any number of mortgagees. Parties may exclude this principle of consolidation in the mortgage deed if they so prefer.

Q23. Describe the rule against inalienability.

Ans: Rule against inalienability. Section-10. Absolute Restraint- The main principle of the T.P Act is that the right to transfer property is incidental to and inseparable from its beneficial ownership. Any condition absolutely restraining alienation is void according to the Act. Section. 10 states that when a property is transferred subject to a condition absolutely restraining the transferee (or any claimant through him) from parting with or disposing of his interest in the property, the condition or limitation is void. This applies to sale, gift, exchange etc. The rule is based on Justice, equity and good conscience, and includes other transfers not covered by the TOPA Act, e.g., will, partition, settlement etc.

Q24. Discuss the Doctrine of Apportionment: Section 36 & 37. And its type

Ans: There are two types of Apportionment:

i. Apportionment by time Section 36- All rents, annuities, pensions, dividends, and other periodical payments, i.e., incomes, when transferred to the transferee, shall be considered accruing from day to day and shall be apportioned accordingly. These are payable on the days appointed for the payment. Execution: This rule does not apply to execution sales made by the Courts.

ii. Apportionment by the Estate Section. 37 -Where as a result of a transfer, the property is divided and held in several shares, and thereupon the benefit of any obligation relating to the property as a whole pass from one to several owners of the property, then law fixes a corresponding duty which shall be performed in favour of each owner in proportion to his share in the property. The duty should be one that can be severed and performed without any burden. Reasonable notice must be given of the severance by the person who is obliged to follow the duty. Exception: This does not apply to leases for agricultural purposes.

Q25. Explain Rule against Accumulation Section 17.

The principle underlying this concept is that property should not be tied up beyond a period fixed by law. The rule against perpetuities is based on a similar principle. Section.17 deals with a direction for valid accumulation. If the terms of property direct that the income from such property shall be accumulated (wholly or in part) during

i. the life of the transferor or

ii. a period of 18 years from the date of the transferor, the direction is valid.

However, if the direction extends beyond the longer of the aforesaid periods, then the direction is invalid. In such a case, the income shall be disposed of, ignoring the direction after the allowed period.

CHAPTER 11

INSOLVENCY AND BANKRUPTCY CODE

The Insolvency and Bankruptcy Code, 2016 was passed to provide a time bound procedure to resolve insolvency among individuals and companies. Insolvency is a condition where an individual or company is incapable to repay its outstanding debt.

The Code defines a financial creditor as someone who has extended any kind of financial credit or loan to the debtor. The Bill elucidates that an allottee under a real estate project (a buyer of an under-construction commercial or residential property) will be considered as a financial creditor. These allottees will be represented on the committee of creditors by an authorized representative who will vote on their behalf.

This committee is responsible for taking key decisions related to the resolution process, such as appointing the resolution professional and approving the resolution plan to be submitted to the National

Company Law Tribunal (NCLT). It also infers that real estate allottees can initiate a corporate insolvency resolution process (CIRP) against the debtor.

Q1. What is the purpose of enactment of the Insolvency and Bankruptcy Code, 2016?

Ans: As per Preamble to the Code, the purpose of this Act is as follows:

a. To consolidate and amend the laws relating to reorganisation and insolvency resolution of corporate persons, partnership firms and individuals.

b. To fix time periods for the execution of the law in a time-bound manner.

c. To make the most of the value of assets of interested persons.

d. To promote entrepreneurship

e. To increase the availability of credit.

f. To balance the interests of all the stakeholders with alteration in the order of significance of payment of Government dues.

g. To establish an Insolvency and Bankruptcy Board of India (IBBI) as a regulatory body for insolvency and bankruptcy law.

Q2. To whom shall the provisions of the Code apply?

Ans: Under Section 2, the provisions of the Code shall apply for insolvency, liquidation, voluntary liquidation or bankruptcy of the following entities:

a. Any company incorporated under the Companies Act, 2013 or under any preceding law.

b. Any other company governed by any special act for the time being in force, except in so far as the said provisions are varying with the provisions of such Special Act.

c. Under the LLP Act 2008, any Limited Liability Partnership

d. Such other body incorporated under any law for the time being in force, as the Central Government may by notification specify in this behalf.

e. Personal Guarantors to Corporate Debtors;

f. Partnership firms and Proprietorship firms;

g. Individuals, besides persons referred to in clause (e).

Q3. What are the services that are included in the term financial service?

Ans: Under section 3(16), Financial services include the following services, specifically:

a. Accepting of deposits

b. Safeguarding and administering assets consisting of financial products, belonging to another person, or agreeing to do so;

c. Effecting contracts of insurance;

d. Managing, Offering, or agreeing to manage assets consisting of financial products belonging to another person;

e. Agreeing or rendering, for consideration, to render advice on or soliciting for the object of—

- Buying, selling, or subscribing to, a financial product;
- Availing a financial service; or
- Exercising any right related with a financial service or financial product;

f. Establishing or operating an investment scheme;

g. Transferring or Maintaining records of ownership of a financial product;

h. Endorsing the issuance or subscription of a financial product; or

   i. Selling, providing, or issuing stored value or payment instruments or providing payment services;

Q4. What shall be considered as Claim under the Code?

Ans: According to Section 3(6) of the Code, Claim means

a. a right to payment, whether or not such right is reduced to judgment, fixed, disputed, undisputed, legal, equitable, secured, or unsecured;

b. right to remedy for breach of contract under any law for the time being in force, if such breach gives rise to a right to payment, whether or not such right is reduced to judgment, fixed, matured, unmatured, disputed, undisputed, secured, or unsecured.

Q5. Who is covered in the definition of person?

Ans: As per Section 3(23) of the Code, a person includes the following:

a. an individual

b. a Hindu Undivided Family

c. a company

d. a trust

e. a partnership

f. A limited liability partnership and any other entity recognized under a statute and comprises a person resident outside India.

Q6. What is the definition of property under the Code?

Ans: As per Section 3(27) of the Code, the property includes: –

a. Money, goods, actionable claims, land and every description of the property, whether situated in India or outside India and,

b. Every description of interest including present or future or vested or contingent interest arising out of, or incidental to, property.

Q7. What is included in the Financial Debt?

Ans: Any amount raised under any other transaction, with any forward sale or purchase agreement, having the commercial outcome of a borrowing.

i. Any amount raised from an allottee under a real estate project shall be deemed to be an amount having the commercial effect of a borrowing; and

ii. The expressions "allottee" and "real estate project" shall have the meaning respectively assigned to them in clauses (d) and (zn) of section 2 of the Real Estate (Regulation and Development) Act, 2016 (16 of 2016).

Q8. What is the time period for the resolution of stressed company under IBC?

Ans:

- The IBC states that the insolvency resolution process must be completed within 180 days, extendable by a period of up to 90 days. As per the act, the resolution process must be completed within 330 days.

- This change is important as many of the resolution cases need more time and if it crosses 330 days, then the company will be liquefied.

Q8. What is the time period for the resolution of stressed company under IBC?

Ans: The IBC states that the insolvency resolution process must be completed within 180 days, extendable by a period of up to 90 days. As per the act, the resolution process must be completed within 330 days.

This change is important as many of the resolution cases need more time and if it crosses 330 days, then the company will be liquefied.

Q9. What is the representation of Financial Creditors?

Ans:

- The Code specifies that when the debt is owed to a class of creditors beyond a specified number, the financial creditors will be represented on the creditors' committee by an authorized representative. These representatives will vote instead of the financial creditors.

- The act states that such representatives will vote based on the decision taken by a majority of the voting share of the creditors that they represent.

- Hence, the act has provided unsecured creditors with a level playing field through the voting framework.

Q10. What is the power and rights of Financial Creditors?

Ans:

- As per the Act, the operational creditors will receive an amount not less than the liquidation value of their debt or the amount that would have been received if the amount had been distributed following the order of priorities of the Code, whichever is higher.
- The Act gives supremacy to financial creditors over operational creditors.
- Moreover, the financial creditors who do not vote in favour of the resolution plan will also receive an amount that is not less than the liquidation value of their debt.

Q11. What is the Committee of Creditors?

Ans:

- Committee of Creditors is a committee consisting of the financial creditors of the Corporate Debtor.
- This Committee eventually forms the decision-making body of the various routine tasks involved in the Corporate Insolvency Resolution Process (CIRP).
- It can be considered like a board of directors a company that approves/ rejects the Resolution Plan (RP), decides upon liquidation of the Corporate Debtor, ratifies expenses borne by the RP, etc.

Q12. How does IBC protect the Home Buyers?

Ans:

- In August 2017, one of the banks took an InfraTech company into insolvency. This caused panic in home buyers regarding whether their rights would be protected or not under IBC Act 2016.

- Before the IBC (Amendment) Act, 2019, if a bank takes a builder/real estate company into insolvency, the priority in giving money back was given to the bank over home buyers.
- This is because the IBC act gives supremacy to financial creditors over operational creditors and Banks are considered as financial creditors.
- After being petitions filed by homebuyers, the Supreme Court gave the order to the government to take steps to protect the rights of home buyers.
- In a subvention scheme, the homebuyer pays 10-20% of the price of the apartment at the time of purchase. A bank pays the balance to the developer as a loan. Although the project is under construction, the developer pays the interest on the loan to the bank. The buyer's EMIs begin only after he/she gets possession.
  - However, many homebuyers/investors were not paid in the Subvention schemes as a builder is not paying the EMI for the subvention plan. Hence, the EMI has to be paid by the buyer instead of the builder in this condition.
  - After the IBC amendments, the homebuyer could have their say in the COC and can get their money back speedily.

Q13. How does IBC protect the Real Estate Company?
Ans:

- The real estate company can defend itself against a bank/homebuyer, taking the company into insolvency. The company can make argument such as:
- The homebuyers did not pay all the instalments.

- The homebuyer is a speculative investor (The investor buys the financial instrument to profit from market price changes).

Q14. How is IBC different from RERA?

Ans:

- From the buyer's perspective, it is better to opt for a resolution process under RERA than to go for liquidation under IBC, as under liquidation, he/she may or may not get their due.
- Under RERA, a builder cannot transfer money from one project to another project. Hence, the builder has to keep most of the money in an escrow account devoted to the project for which he has raised money.
- It cannot be considered the duplication, as, under RERA, banks and financial institutions have the capabilities to unlawfully seize the whole proceeds of the recovery of the money from defaulting company. In this scenario, the homebuyers had to wait forever and might not get their money.
- Moreover, RERA is not so much dealing with creditors at large.

Q15. Which assets shall not be used for recovery in liquidation?

Ans: The subsequent assets shall not be used for recovery in the liquidation:

- Any assets owned by a third party, which own a corporate debtor, and which include-
- Assets held in trust for any third party
- Bailment contracts

- All sums due to any employee or workman from the provident fund, the gratuity fund and pension fund
- Other contractual arrangements which do not specify transfer of title but only use of the assets
- Such other assets may be notified by the Central Government in consultation with any financial sector regulator.
- Assets in security collateral held by financial services providers and are subject to set-off and netting in multi-lateral clearing or trading transactions;
- Personal assets of any partner of corporate debtor or shareholder as the case may be provided such assets are not held on account of evasion transactions that may be avoided under this Chapter;
- Assets of any Indian or foreign subsidiary of the corporate debtor; or
- Any other assets as may be stated by the Board, with assets which could be subject to set-off on account of mutual dealings between any creditor and the corporate debtor

Q16. What are the advantages available for homebuyer under IBC?

Ans:

- Expeditious Remedy
- Summary Procedure
- Limited defence available to the builder
- Builders distress the loss of control of the company and possible investigations and hence settle faster.

- IRP has sufficient power to request NCLT for investigations into fund siphoning, preferential or fraudulent transactions etc. and revive the company
- Even projects which have ruined can be revived through an effective resolution plan
- Can overlook unfair terms in the agreement and pass orders in the interest of justice
- Physical as well as e-courts systems
- Relatively quicker proceeding than regular civil or consumer proceedings
- Sufficient powers to issue directions, direct payment of compensation with interest and imposition of penalties
- Power to order payment of punitive damages.

Q17. What are the limitations for homebuyer under IBC?

Ans:

- The minimum threshold of 100 buyers or 10% buyers tough to satisfy.
- Provisional suspension of Code and enhanced default limit of 1 crore
- The default must be crystal clear and there should not be any contributory default from the buyer's end.
- Documentation of debt and default must be well kept
- The relatively softer stand taken by RERA authorities
- RERA authority appointment and functioning not constant across India.

- No fear of consequence among erring builders.
- Builder can postpone or delay proceedings by approaching Civil Courts
- Cannot easily overlook the terms of the written agreement even when they are unfair to some extent.

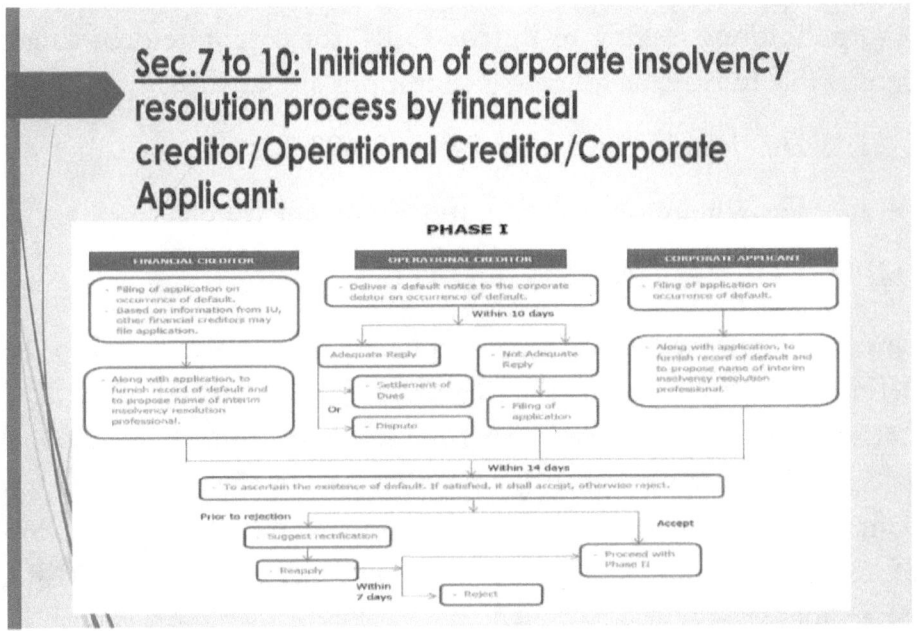

Q18. Recent Amendments in IBC

Ans: Under the said powers vested in him under the Constitution of India, the Hon'ble President of India has promulgated the IBC Ordinance 2020 on 05.06.2020 to effectively suspend the operation of Sections 7, 9 & 10 of the Insolvency and Bankruptcy Code, 2016 relating to defaults arising on or after 25.03.2020 for six months, extensible up to a maximum of one year from such date as may be notified. The declaration of this Ordinance has resulted in the addition of new clauses, i.e., Section 10A and Section 66(3) into the Insolvency and Bankruptcy Code, 2016.

The instant Ordinance also assuages the creditors' fear to a great extent by clearly enunciating that the newly inserted provision of Section 10A shall not apply to any defaults that were committed before 25.03.2020. Therefore, creditors would be allowed to file applications under S. 7, 9, and 10 of the IBC, 2016 in case the corporate debtor committed any defaults in payments before 25.03.2020.

Applications seeking to initiate CIRP for corporate debtors are permissible in case the following conditions are satisfied:

i. The default which arose before 25.03.2020

ii. The amount of default is more than Rs. 1 crore.

IMPACT OF IBC ON REAL ESTATE

Under the current ordinance, an explanation has been added to the definition of "financial debt" given under Section 5(8)(f) of the IBC Act, whereby 'financial debt' has been redefined to include 'allottee' as defined under section 2(d) of RERA and 'real estate project' as defined in section 2(zn) of RERA. When anyone sees the definition of 'real estate project', 'allottee', 'building' 'apartment' under RERA it becomes clear that –

- An 'allottee' means a person to whom a 'plot', building 'or 'apartment' has been allotted. 'Apartment' itself has been defined under section 2(e) of RERA to include a flat, office, etc., whether for a residential or commercial purpose.

- Similarly, 'building' under section 2(j) of the RERA has been defined to include any structure, whether for residential or commercial use. The fact that the legislature has preferred to include the definition of allottee from RERA relatively than any other legislation would necessarily need that the terms contained in section 2(d) of RERA such as building, apartment, etc. would also have to be taken as defined in the RERA and not from any other legislation. Therefore, it would indicate that residential and commercial properties are included within the meaning of the term allottee.

- Since the term 'allottee' as defined under section 2(d) of RERA itself provides that it includes a person who has subsequently acquired the said allotment through sale or transfer suggests that second allottees or person buying it in resale are also to be considered as 'financial creditors' for the Insolvency Act.

- An interpretation of the definition of 'real estate project' as defined under section 2(zn) read with section 2(d) of RERA seems to specify that not only the apartment, building or plot but even the common areas, other development works, structures, improvements, and elementary rights and appurtenances belonging thereto get included within the domain of rights being protected for the allottees.

The fact that consumers can now approach the NCLT for insolvency proceedings or be treated as financial creditors in case an Insolvency Resolution Professional has been appointed is a massive step forward for safeguarding the interests of the consumers. Having said that, there is an interesting and intricate relationship between the rights of the consumers/ allottees under Insolvency proceedings as compared to RERA and another issue that would need to be resolved is at what stage and under what situations would an Allottee be allowed to invoke the provisions of the Insolvency Code considering the definition of 'default' as given under the Insolvency Code as compared to RERA.

CHAPTER 12

GST AND CAPITAL GAINS

1. Goods and Services Tax (GST) became effective in July 2017 and it has been a distinct advantage over all areas of our economy, Real Estate being one of the bigger divisions. Intended to get rid of the various taxes like VAT, Administration tax, and others, it has surely helped build an increasingly rearranged and vigorous tax framework.

2. Real estate is one of the most significant parts of the Indian economy and records 6-8% of its Gross domestic product. With the execution of GST, the nation stands to observe some noteworthy changes in this area.

3. With significant relaxations in some serious sections of the real estate industry, similar to the rental markets, these portions saw a spike in investing activity while others remained generally steady. The effect of GST on real estate has been remarkable.

4. Real estate, which used to be taxed at the pace of 12%, is presently taxed at the rate of 5% and real estate goliaths accept that this assemblage of taxes into one unit has, in reality, helped support the segment and quicken development.

5. Although taxes, for example, Stamp Obligation and Registration charges, and those related to development materials stay independent, GST still assists with uniting a composite arrangement of taxing with some rewarding advantages in this segment. In this way, boosting interests in this area, especially in the Rental Markets, particularly on

account of properties leased for private purposes. **What is a residential real estate project?**

A Real Estate Undertaking in which the floor covers the business space region is not over 15% of all flats' all-out carpet area region in the project.

6. **What is an affordable residential apartment?**

   An affordable project for the residential apartment is one in which:

   - Carpet region area is up to 60 square meters for urban cities;
   - Carpet area is up to 90 – square meter for cities and towns other than urban cities and;
   - The total gross amount summed up by the project builder is not more than Rs.45 Lakhs.

   For E.g., Mr A is a beneficiary of PMAY – CLSS and the carpet area of his flat being under construction is 150 square meters. Is he eligible for a new tax rate of 1%?

   Yes, only if the developer has not exercised the option to pay tax at old rates. Here, the area in the square meter is greater than the prescribed limits, but it is still considered as an affordable residential apartment because Mr A is a beneficiary of PMAY CLSS.

7. **What is an ongoing project?**

   A project is considered as an ongoing project if the following conditions are satisfied:

   1. Where Commencement Certificate is required and has been given by the skilled expert at the very latest 31st March 2019 and the equivalent is ensured by an enrolled registered architect, sanctioned architect, or an authorized assessor that

the development of the undertaking began at the very latest 31st March 2019.

E.g. In the event of a sole tower including 50 stories and enlisted as a single venture, separate initiation declarations might be given by the Competent Authority. If one or two certificates are received on or before 31st March 2019 and some later, the same is still considered as an ongoing under-construction project.

2. A CC where not mandatory to be duly issued by the competent authority, then the same shall be issued by a registered architect, chartered engineer, or a licensed surveyor that the project's construction started on or before 31st March 2019.

3. CC is not given on or before 31st March 2019.

   For instance, if a project has three blocks and a completion certificate is received for one block before 1st April 2019 and the rest are received after this date. In such a case, the project is considered as an ongoing project because, as per the Notification issued by Government, a project is considered complete only if the Completion Certificate is issued for the entire project and not a part thereof.

   The 1st occupation of the venture/project has not taken place before 31st March 2019.

   For instance, if an occupation certificate is received only for a part of the premises (up to 31st March 2019) in a huge project and not the entire project, the same is considered as an ongoing project.

4. Apartments are wholly booked or partly booked on or before 31st March 2019.

E.g. 1. This condition is not applicable for the redevelopment of slum rehabilitation projects as the beneficiaries, in this case, are not mandatory to pay any pecuniary consideration for flats allotted to them.

Note: A project where bookings have not started but the construction has started before 31st March 2019 will not be considered an 'ongoing project'. It will be treated as a new project and the new tax rates will apply

8. **What are the new GST rates on the construction of residential apartments?**

Below are the new tax rates without ITC for housing projects applicable w.e.f 1.4.2019

Rate	Description
1%	New affordable housing projects
	Ongoing affordable housing projects opting for new rates
5%	Ongoing other than affordable housing projects
	New, other than affordable housing projects
	Projects with commercial space <15% of total carpet area

Conditions to be satisfied for availing the above rates:

i. **ITC:** ITC cannot be claimed.

ii. **Purchase of inputs from registered persons:** At Least 80% of the total value of inputs and input services should be purchased from registered suppliers.

However, the value of the following services used in the construction of residential apartments are excluded from this calculation:

- Grant of developmental rights
- Elongated period lease of land
- FSI
- Value of electricity
- charge of ultra-speed diesel
- Natural gas and Motor spirit

The promoter should pay GST @18% on reverse charge mechanism on all such internal supplies to the degree shy of 80% of internal supplies from enrolled provider aside from concrete on which tax must be paid at 28% (whenever bought from unregistered people).

9. **Does a promoter or a builder have the option to pay tax at old 8% & 12% rates with ITC?**

Yes, in the case of an ongoing project, a promoter or builder can exercise a one-time option to pay tax at old rates. This should be communicated to the Jurisdictional Commissioner by 20th May 2019 in the prescribed form. If not communicated, it is deemed that they have opted for making tax payments at new rates. Also, modification of options is not allowed once submitted.

Note:

1. This option needs to be exercised for each ongoing project separately. Along these lines, promoters may practice various alternatives for various continuous ventures embraced by him.

2. This option is also available for specific schemes like PMAY, Housing For All, RAY, or any other Central or State Government housing schemes.

3. This option can be exercised by a promoter or a builder and not the buyer.

10. **What are the GST rates on TDR, FSI and long-term lease of land?**

Transfer of development rights or FSI by way of an agreement on or before 31st March 2019 is exempted from tax even if the money for the same is paid (cash or kind) in part or full on or after 1st April 2019. Below are the tax rates:

a. If the supply of TDR, FSI, or elongated term lease of the land is used for the building of residential flats, Tax on TDR is to be computed based on the following formula: GST is applicable on such rate which is in proportion to the building of residential flats that remain un-booked on the date of issue of CC/first occupation. The tax rate is 18%, subject to a tax amount that is limited to 1% or 5% of the value of flats depending upon whether the TDR/FSI is used for an affordable residential flat or other than an affordable residential flat.

b. If the supply of TDR, FSI, or long-term lease of land is used for the construction of business-related offices: GST at 18%.

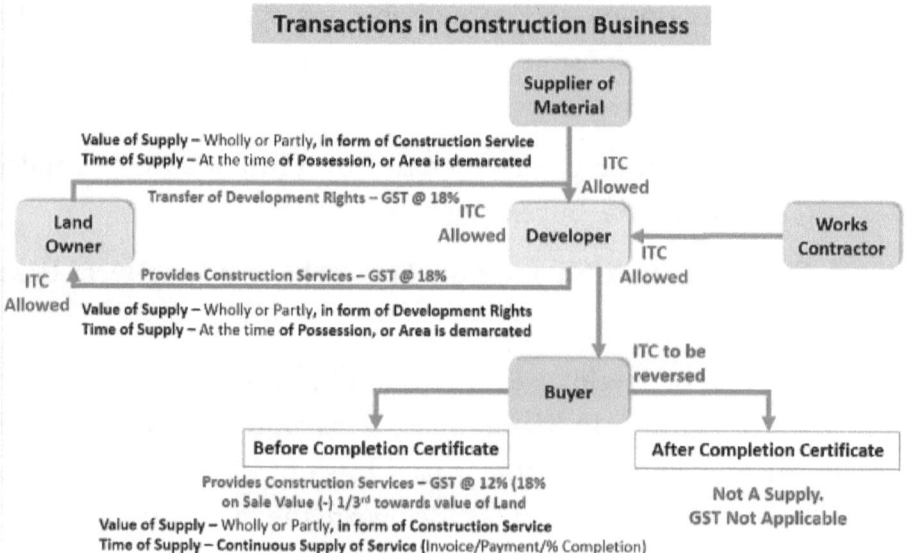

11. Who is liable to pay GST on TDR and floor space index?

The promoter is obligated to pay GST on the reverse charge mechanism on TDR or FSI provided on or after first April 2019. Regardless of whether a landowner is not occupied with a normal business of land-related exercises, the move of development rights by such a person to the promoter is obligated to GST as it is considered supplying of service under Sec 7 of CGST Act.

Also, in the case of outward supply of TDR by one developer to another, GST is applicable at 18% on reverse charge.

12. At what point in time, the promoter should discharge its tax liability on the supply of TDR, FSI and long-term lease?

Description	Point of taxation
TDR	The liability to pay tax arises on the date of execution or first control of the venture, whichever is prior. Thus, GST would be applied on the charge, which is in proportion to the construction of a residential apartment that remains unbooked on the date of issue of CC/first occupation.
FSI	**For FSI received after 1st April 2019:** **If consideration for FSI is in the type of development of the business or private flats –** accountability arises on the date of issuance of CC. **If consideration for FSI is in monetary form–** • For Residential Apartment Construction: Liability arises on the date of issuance of CC. • For Commercial Apartment Constructions: Liability to pay tax shall arise immediately.
Long term lease	**For long term lease received after 1st April 2019:** type of development of the business or private condos Risk emerges on the date of issuance of the Finish Testament in the development of private flats. Be that as it may, the risk to pay tax will emerge promptly if such long-haul rent is identified with business space.

13. What is the classification and rate of tax on works contract service provided by a contractor to a developer or promoter under the new scheme?

- Affordable Housing Project – 12%, provided affordable housing space is more than 50% of the total carpet area.
- Residential housing project Other than Affordable housing – 18%
- Commercial Housing -18%

14. Are there Any Tax Advantages for Non-Resident Indians purchasing properties?

No tax benefits are accessible for NRI's except if you document your profits and, in this way, get qualified to profit from the tax benefits.

15. Whether Rental Pay could be charged to tax in possession of an individual who is anything but a registered proprietor of a property?

Rental pay from a property is charged to tax under the head "Income from house property in possession of the proprietor of the property". If an individual accepting the lease is not the proprietor of the property, at that point rental payment is not charged to tax under the head "Income from house property" (For example, Lease got by an occupant from sub-letting). In the accompanying cases, an individual may not be the enrolled proprietor of the property. However, he will be treated like the proprietor (i.e., regarded proprietor) of the property, and rental payments from the property will be charged to tax in his grasp:

If an individual exchanges their home property to his/her life partner (not being an exchange regarding consent to live separated) or to his/her minor kids (not being married girl) without satisfactory consideration, at that point, the transferor will be esteemed as proprietor of the property.

1. Holder of the impartible estate is esteemed as the proprietor of the property included in the estate

2. An individual from co-operative society, organization, or other relationship of people to whom a structure (or some portion of it) is allocated or rented under house building plan of the general public, organization or relationship, by and large, is treated as considered proprietor of the property.

3. An individual getting property by fulfilling the states of segment 53A of the Transfer of Property Act will be treated as the considered proprietor (in spite of the fact that he may not be the enlisted proprietor). Area 53A of said Act endorses the following conditions:

    a. There must be an understanding recorded as a hard copy.

    b. The consideration for purchase is paid, or the buyer is happy to pay it.

    © Buyer has taken ownership of the property incompatibility of the understanding.

3. if there should be an occurrence of rent of a property for a period surpassing 12 years (regardless of whether initially fixed or arrangement for augmentation exists), the resident is esteemed to be the proprietor of the property. Be that as it may, any privilege by the method of rent from month to month or for a period not surpassing one year is not secured by this arrangement.

16. **Under what head is rental income from the shop charged to tax?**

   To tax the rental income under the head "Income from house property", the rented property should be building or land appurtenant thereto. Shop being a building, rental income will be charged to tax under the head "Income from house property".

17. **How is rental income from one's property treated for the purpose of taxation?**

   Income from Rentals must be taxed under the head "income from house property". The deduction is accessible under Section 23 and 24 of the Income Tax Act.

   It might be noticed that a conclusion is accessible for fixes, whether acquired or not. Real costs are deductible with the exception of a favourable rate.

18. **How can investors optimise their long-term/short-term capital gains tax liability?**

   Financial specialists can limit/decrease LTCG by either putting resources into capital increases bonds or by putting resources into private house property under the arrangements of Section 54, 54F and 54EC of the Income-tax Act, 1961.

   STCG can be balanced against momentary capital misfortunes.

Advantages of GST

- GST has joined various taxes like Central Excise, Sales Tax, Service Tax, Luxury Tax, and so on and presented to everything under one rooftop. This has disentangled the tax count and assortment process.

- GST has improved the straightforwardness of the tax assortment process.

- Industry specialists accept that the expenses of goods and services will descend over the long haul due to GST, this is on the grounds that prior various Worth Included Tax (Tanks) made the cost of goods and services blow up. Presently, one single tax will destroy that issue.

- Service suppliers, who have a turnover of under Rs.20 lakh, need not pay GST. In North-Eastern states, the limit is lower – Rs.10 lakh. This is a major favourable position for private ventures, as they can maintain a strategic distance from the tedious taxation process and rather centre around their business exercises.

- GST will likewise bring genuinely necessary responsibility and guidelines to sloppy areas, for example, the material business. In India, sloppy divisions give enormous scope work and create gigantic income. However, they are very indiscriminate with regards to tax responsibility. GST tries to address this inconsistency.

- Under the current taxation framework, there are isolated taxes for goods and services. For this, the exchange esteems must be isolated into estimations of goods and services to decide tax obligation. This outcome in increased entanglements and organization migraines. GST will kill this.

- Earlier, the legislature confronted the intricate undertaking of dealing with numerous circuitous taxes. Yet, the foundation of the GST, the GST System (GSTN), will deal with all the procedures identified with GST activity. This is a completely incorporated stage, which will disentangle and guarantee the smooth working of the GST exercises.

- GST will be exacted distinctly at the last goal of utilization, subsequently evacuating two-fold taxation at numerous focuses from maker to retailer outlets. This is a stage towards annihilating financial twists.

- Many feel that the general effect of GST has exceptionally affected this division, while some accept that the upsides and downsides have adjusted one another and that there has been no considerable change.

CHAPTER 13

REGISTRATION AND STAMP ACT

Registration of the property is a full and final agreement signed between two parties. Once a property is registered, it implies that the property purchaser in whose favour the property is enlisted is the is the lawful owner of the premises and is fully responsible for it in all respects. The law does not recognize unregistered owners and does not give them any rights over the property. Therefore, Registration of Property is Compulsory to prevent fraud or future litigation.

Whenever a property buyer buys a piece of land/immovable property, he/she needs to register the same with authority concerned. Once a property is registered, it implies that the property purchaser in whose favor the property is registered is the legitimate owner of the premises and is completely answerable for it in all regards. Through the **registration of the sale deed**, a person can acquire the rights of the property on the date of execution of the deed.

Registering the documents relating to the transfer, sale, lease, or any other property disposal form is compulsory under section 17 of the Indian Registration Act, 1908. The registration aim is to prevent fraud, in addition to create and maintain an up-to-date public record. *The registration can occur at the Sub-Registration Office within which the property is located or in the District Sub-Registrar Office of the District where the property is located.*

According to Section 17 of the Registration Act 1908, all operations involving the sale of land that exceeds Rs100 should be registered. This implies that all sales of real estate transactions must be registered, as no real estate can be bought for Rs 100. Furthermore, all transactions concerning gifts of real estate and rentals of more than 12 months also require registration.

The paperwork involved in a real estate transaction, including stamp duty on property buy that you need to pay, involves a decent measure of cash getting spent. All things considered, it is these papers that remain as confirmation of your property possession. Among the major costs are the one-time registration fee and stamp duty that you have to pay under Section 3 of the Indian Stamp Duty Act, 1899, after a sale deed is processed.

Stamp duty rate: The rates at which stamp duty is charged in various Indian states at present range from 4 per cent to 10 per cent. Registration fees, on the other hand, stand at a standard of one per cent across states.

Payment frequency and penalty: Stamp duty is a one-time charge paid under Section 3 of the Indian Stamp Duty Act, 1899. If you fail to pay this charge, you have to pay the outstanding amount along with a penalty of two per cent of the outstanding amount per month. The penalty could go to as high as 200 per cent of the original liability.

Stamp duty on the purchase of apartments: Apartment buyers have to pay stamp duty charges based on the individual share of the property. This means if a project is built on 50,000 sq ft of land and units of similar sizes are sold to 10 people, each one of them has to pay a stamp duty charge for 5,000 sq ft.

Documentary evidence: In case of a dispute, the document showing you have paid the stamp duty acts as legal proof of your ownership over the property. It ought to be noticed that property registration papers are not considered legitimate evidence; they just demonstrate that you paid an expense. This has also been a reason why many homebuyers put the property registration work on the back burner. Nonetheless, in the event that you need to sell your property later on, it will be hard for you to do as such if the registration has not been finished.

State subject: Though regulated by a Central Act – The Indian Stamp Duty Act, 1899 – stamp duty charges are collected by states, and these form a crucial part of their revenue collections. States have the Constitutional option to roll out any improvements to the Act and have their own arrangements of rules in such manner. Stamp duty charges vary across states. Additionally, even in a specific state, they may fluctuate starting with one area then onto the next. Maharashtra, for instance, has the Bombay Stamp Act, 1958, which regulates stamp duty and property registration in the state. Other states like Gujarat, Karnataka, Kerala, Rajasthan and Tamil Nadu also have their stamp duty laws.

Homebuyers in India sometimes put off property registration because of high stamp duty charges. This severely hits the government's revenue collection and may also be a reason why land and property transaction records are in a poor state. Compared with other economies, stamp duty charges in India are high. According to a World Bank report, the countries like Philippines and Vietnam charge stamp duty in the range of one to two per cent.

1. **Is property registration mandatory?**

    As per Section 17 of the Registration Act, 1908, all transactions that involve the sale of immovable property for a value exceeding Rs 100 should be registered. This effectively means that all the transactions of sale of immovable property have to be merely Rs 100. Additionally, all transactions of the gift of immovable property and lease for a period exceeding 12 months are also mandatorily required to be registered.

In special cases, when a party to the transaction cannot come to the sub-registrar's office, the sub-registrar may depute any of its officers to accept the documents for registration at the residence of such person. The term 'immovable property' includes land, buildings and any rights attached to these properties.

Under the provisions of the Act, the registration of these property documents is a must:

- Documents regarding the gift of immovable property.

- Documents that are created to "create, declare, assign, limit or extinguish" any right, title or interest of the value of Rs 100 and upwards in an immovable property.

- Leases of immovable property that are for one year or more.

- Documents that are created after a court order transferring any right, title or interest of the value of Rs 100 and upwards in an immovable property.

SEC. 17 - DOCUMENTS WHOSE REGISTRATION IS COMPULSORY

a. Instruments of gift of immovable property.
b. Other non-testamentary instruments [Other than instruments of Gift of immovable property]
c. Non-testamentary instruments which purport to create, declare, assign, limit or extinguish, whether in present or in future, any such right, title or interest whether vested or contingent, of the value of Rs. 100/- and above.
d. Leases of immovable property from year to year or any term exceeding one year or reserving a yearly rent.
e. Non-testamentary instruments transferring or assigning any decree or order of a court or any award in order to create interests as mentioned in clause (c).

2. Registration of what documents are optional?

In certain cases, registration of documents is optional. These include:

- Documents, other than instruments of gift and wills, which purport or operate to create, declare, assign, limit or extinguish any right, title or interest of a value less than Rs 100 in an immovable property.

- Leases of immovable property for any term not exceeding one year. Registration for leases that are exempted under Section 17 is also optional.

- Documents created after a court order transfer any right, title, or interest of the value of less than Rs 100 in an immovable property.

- Will

3. Which are the documents requires to be compulsorily registered?

1. Gift deed of immovable property.

2. Other non-testamentary instruments, which purport or Operate to create, declare, assign, limit or extinguish whether in the present or future, any right, title or interest, whether vested or contingent, of the value of one hundred rupees and upwards, to or in immovable property. E.g., Sale, mortgage, partition, release, settlement of the immovable property.

3. Non- testamentary instruments which acknowledge the receipt or payment of any consideration on account of the creation, declaration, assignment, limitation or extension of any such right, title or interest;

4. Leases of immovable property

5. Non – testamentary instruments transferring or assigning any decree or order of a court or any award when such decree or order or award purports or operates to create, declare, assign, limit or extinguish whether in the present or future, any right, title or interest, whether vested or contingent, of the value of one hundred rupees and upwards, to or in immovable property;

6. The documents containing contracts to transfer for consideration, any immovable property under section 53A of the Transfer of Property Act, 1882 shall be registered if they have been executed on or after the commencement of the Registration and Other Related Laws (Amendment) Act, 2000 and if such documents are not registered on or after such commencement, then, they shall not affect the said section 53A

4. What property documents need not be registered?

Certain property-related documents, as specified under the Act, need not be registered. These include:

- A grant of immovable property by the government.

- Any order made under the Charitable Endowments Act, 1890, vesting any property in a treasurer of charitable endowments or divesting any such treasurer of any property.

- Property purchased at a public auction where a civil or a revenue officer is the seller.

5. What if there are false statements made in documents?

Section 82 of the Act says that imprisonment for up to seven years or a fine (no specific amount is mentioned in this regard) or both could be imposed in case a buyer "intentionally makes any false statements present a false copy or translation of a document or a map or plan". Attempts to "falsely personates other people is also a punishable offence.

6. **Who is responsible for fixing property registration charges?**

   State governments fix stamp duty and registration charges. While stamp duty charges vary from state to state (within a range of 4-10 per cent of the transaction value), a buyer has to pay one per cent of the deal value as registration charges.

   Aside from fixing the over two charges, states additionally fix charges for looking for the registers (on the off chance that you need to discover something from the records), make or grant copies of reasons, entries, or documents before, on or after registration. They also decide the additional fees payable for the issue of commissions, for filing translations, for attending at private residences and for the safe custody and return of documents.

7. **What is the purpose of Registration?**

   When the registration is made, it puts a mark that it is permanent and is on public record. It is mandatory to register the transaction because it is only when you can avail the rights under TOPA.

8. **Is there a time limit to present a document for registration after it is executed (signed)?**

   a. The document may be presented for registration within four months from the date of execution (signature).

   b. If a document is executed out of India, the period of four months will be counted from the date of its first receipt in India.

c. After four months document may be presented within another four months with a penalty subject to a maximum of ten times the registration fees if the District Registrar grants permission. But document may be presented before Sub Registrar within eight months. Thereafter it cannot be accepted for registration.

9. **What is the course if the executing party refuses to appear in Registry Office to admit execution?**

   In such circumstances, registering office will issue notice/summons to the Executant. If the party does not turn up registering officer will refuse registration.

   a. Application may be made to the District Registrar on such refusal. The District Registrar will hold an enquiry and decide the case. A prescribed fee should be paid for such an application.

   b. One may submit an appeal to the Civil Court if District Registrar also refuses to order for registration

10. **Who can sign as a witness to a document?**

    The Person signing the document should be major, i.e. above 18yrs

11. **Explain the Power of Attorney?**

    There are two kinds of Power of Attorney.

    1. General Power of Attorney (GPA)
    2. Special Power of Attorney (SPA)
    3. Special Power of Attorney requires attestation (As per Sec 32 and 33 of Registration Act)

a. A person executes general Power of Attorney in favour of another to act on behalf of him generally. It may include management of property, Court matter/litigations, sale or mortgage of property or any other act.

b. Special Power of Attorney is executed to do a particular act.

c. Special Power of Attorney authorizing the agent to present the document executed by the Principal before the Registering Officer concerned and admit the execution thereof, requires to be attested by the Sub Registrar/Registrar in case the Principal resides in India except in Jammu and Kashmir. If the principal resides in Jammu and Kashmir, then it has to be attested by the Magistrate. And if the principal resides outside India, then the power shall be attested by Consul/vice-Consul/Notary Public/Magistrate.

Power of Attorney holder is answerable to the principal and liable to give accounts to him.

12. Where can I register my immovable property?

It should be registered in the Sub-Registrar office in your local boundaries. For any reason, there is a problem with the sub-registrar office, and then the party can approach the "District Registrar" of your district under "Section 30 of Registration Act" to get it registered through his Joint I SR.

13. What is meant by Encumbrance Certificate?

It is that certificate that shows the record of the property. Assume if there is a deal, contract or different deeds concerning the immovable property, at that point in such case ordering is made and this ordering is changed over to produce an encumbrance certificate.

14. **Explain the term Special Power of Attorney?**

It simply means that the power is transferred to another person to act on his behalf, only for a special purpose.

The person appointed can carry on function on behalf of the person who has given the authority and such power of attorney should be authenticated or attested by a Sub Registrar. If they are not then it is not accepted for registration.

15. **If private property was wrongly shown by revenue or any other department as falling under Prohibited property under Section 22A, then what is the remedy?**

In such a situation, the party should contact the office of the revenue department or any other authorized department and then the party should submit the property documents to show that it is private.

After the inspection by the authority, they may issue NOC or may send a new list to the department where the registration is made stating that the property in question is private.

INDIAN STAMP ACT, 1899

Q1. Discuss about Stamp Duties?

Ans: As mentioned under the act, the following instruments are to be charged with the respective duties as mentioned under the act/schedule. The Instruments are as follows:

- Any Instrument that has not been executed by any person previously;
- Instruments such as promissory notes, bills of exchange etc.
- Any other instruments other than promissory notes, bills of exchange that are mentioned under the schedule mentioned under the act.

Q2. Discuss wherein there should not be any duty charged?

Ans: The following Instruments should not be charged any duty as mentioned under the act are as follows:

- Any instruments executed on behalf or in favour of any government department;
- Any Instrument for sale/transfer of any ship or any vessel.

Q3. Discuss about the Instruments used in the transaction of sale/mortgage/settlement?

Ans: As under section 4 of the act in the case of any sale/mortgage/settlement, different types of instruments are used for completing the transaction, the principal instrument only shall be chargeable with the duty prescribed in Schedule I, and each of the other instruments shall be chargeable with a duty of one rupee instead of the duty prescribed for it in that Schedule.

Q4. Discuss about instruments related to distinct matter?

Ans: As under section 5 of the Act, the instruments comprising of distinct matters shall be charged with the aggregate amount of the duties.

Q5. Discuss about the adjudication of stamps?

Ans: As referenced under the demonstration, when any instrument, if executed, is brought to the Collector, and the individual bringing it applies to have the assessment of that official with respect to the obligation which is chargeable and pays an expense of such sum. Post which the Collector will guarantee by support on such instrument that the full obligation which is chargeable has been paid.

Q6. Discuss about the offences that are mentioned under the act?

Ans: As mentioned under the act, the penalty for the execution of an instrument that is not stamped is a fine that amounts to Rs. 500/-.

CHAPTER 14

MODEL TENANCY LAWS

The Model Tenancy Act lays down the obligations of tenants and landlords and provides for an adjudication mechanism for disputes. The existing rent control laws are restricting the growth of rental housing and discourage owners from renting out their vacant houses due to fear of repossession. One of the potential measures to unlock the vacant house is to bring transparency and accountability to the existing system of renting of premises and balance the interests of both the property owner and the tenant in a judicious manner.

The Model Act lays down the obligations of tenants and landlords and provides for an adjudication mechanism for disputes. The Act mandates that no person will let or take any rental premises without an agreement in writing in both urban and rural areas. Within two months of executing such an agreement, the landowner and tenant are required to intimate the Rent Authority, who will issue a unique identification number to both parties. Agreements can be submitted through a dedicated digital platform. The act is beautiful legislation that deals in rental matters. As mentioned under the act, the Establishment of the adjudicating authorities will help lower the burden on lower courts in the country in matters relating to tenancy.

Q1. What is the objective behind bringing such a beautiful piece of legislation?

Ans: The main intention of getting the act into the picture was to balance the owner and the tenants' interests for any such disputes that arose between them and to redress the disputes between them.

Q2. Discuss about premises as mentioned under the act?

Ans: Under section 2(E) of the Model Tenancy Act premises means a building or a part of the building which is used for residences or commercial purposes or educational purpose.

Q3. Discuss about the Agreement made by a landlord as mentioned under the Act?

Ans: As mentioned under the act, the agreement which the landlord executes is a tenancy agreement.

Q4. Describe the tenancy agreement as mentioned under the Act?

Ans: A tenancy agreement is a written agreement that is executed by the landlord while providing a space for rent to a tenant. The landlord and the tenant must inform about such agreement which is executed between them to the rent authority and in such form as prescribed under the act.

Q5. Discuss about the time limit for informing the rent authority about the tenancy agreement?

Ans: As decided under section 4 of the model tenancy act, both the landlord and tenant must inform about such agreement to the rent authority and in such form as prescribed under the Act within 2 months after execution of such Act.

Q6. Describe the duties of rent authorities upon receiving such information about the tenancy agreement?

Ans: the duties of rent authorities upon receiving such information about the tenancy agreement are as follows-

- Provide a unique identification number for such tenancy agreement;
- Upload the details of such agreement in the state language where such agreement is executed.

The whole things need to be completed in 7 days.

Q7. Can the information provided under such agreement be used as evidence in the court of law?

Ans: As per section 4(5), yes, the information provided under such agreement can be used as evidence in the court of law.

Q8. Describe the period of tenancy as mentioned under the act?

Ans: The period of tenancy between the landlord and tenants can be for a period as discussed between them before the execution of such agreements.

Q9. Can the Tenancy agreement go for a renewal or extension?

Ans: Yes, under section5 (2), the tenant can ask the landlord for a renewal or extension before the expiry of the previous agreement which was executed between them.

Q10. Describe the consequences of the tenancy agreement which was for a fixed term gets expired?

Ans: After the fixed term agreement expires and if the tenant has not vacated the premises to the landlord, it is deemed to be on a month to month basis on the terms and conditions that were decided earlier and only for six months.

Q11. Does the act provide any rights and duties to the successors of both landlord and tenants?

Ans: Yes as per section 6 of the act, it provides any rights and duties to the successors of both landlord and tenants. It says that the successors will have the same rights and obligations as mentioned in the agreement for the remaining period.

Q12. Discuss about the restrictions on subletting of premises by the tenants?

Ans: As per section 7 of the act, a tenant without taking prior permission from the landlord cannot sublet the premises to a third party.

Q13. What is to be done by a tenant in case of subletting a premise?

The tenant shall notify the landowner about the complete details of subletting and rent and security payable by him.

Q14. Discuss about the rent payable under the act?

Ans: As per section 8 of the act, the rent payable by the tenant is the amount that is decided mutually between them at the time of entering into the agreement.

Q15. Discuss about the revision of rent under the act?

Ans: The revision of rent between the landlord and the tenant as per the terms set out in the Tenancy Agreement. Under sec.9 (2), the landlord shall provide a notice to the tenant in writing 3 months before he wants to hike the rent.

Q16. How can a revision be made on a fixed-term tenancy agreement?

Ans: As per sec.9 (4), rent may not be hiked during the current tenancy period unless the increase is expressly set out in the Tenancy Agreement.

Q17. Can the rent authority fix or revise the mutually decided rent?

Ans: As per the act, The Rent Authority on an application by the landlord or tenant, will fix or revise the rent and also let them know about the dates from which the revised rent will be payable.

Q18. Discuss about the Security Deposit under the Act?

Ans: As per the act, the tenant's security deposit is paid in advance as agreed by both parties. It is subject to two month's rent in the case of residential property and one month in the case of non-residential property.

Q19. Discuss about the agreement to be given to the tenant?

Ans: After the execution of such agreement, the landlord must give a signed copy of such agreement to the tenant within 15 days in the manner mentioned under the act.

Q20. Discuss about the receipt to be given for the rent paid?

Ans: Under the act, every tenant shall pay rent and other charges payable within the stipulated time as mutually agreed.

Q21. Discuss about the duties of a tenant during a tenancy?

Ans: During the tenancy, the tenant must -
- not intentionally or negligently damage the premises or permit such damage;

- notify the landowner of any damage as soon as possible;
- Take care of the premises and their contents including fitting and fixtures.

Appendix: State Real Estate Laws

On the following pages are state listings containing relevant information regarding real estate and landlord/tenant law. You are advised to check your state's listing carefully to determine the particular requirements in your jurisdiction. Every state has some differing requirements. Following is an explanation of the listings:

State Landlord-Tenant Statutes: This listing provides a reference to the statute book location that contains each particular state's laws regarding landlord/tenant relations.

State Property Law Statutes: Should you wish to research the law in your state, this lists the name and chapter of the state statute in which the laws regarding real property are found in each state.

State web address: This listing notes the internet web address of each state's online website. For most state sites, you will arrive at the main index for the state and will need to locate the specific site for the state's statute/legislative information by using the references in the listings above, *State Landlord-Tenant Statutes* and *State Property Law Statutes*. These websites were current at the time of this appendice's publication.

State Real Estate Disclosure Laws: This listing specifies the name of the document that is required to be completed by a seller disclosing their knowledge about the property for sale. At press time, 32 states had provided some type of statutory real estate disclosure form. Also noted is the statutory location of real estate disclosure laws.

Landlord's Entry to Real Estate: This listing provides the state requirement surrounding the right of a landlord to enter a rented property.

Security Deposit Amount Limits: Under this listing are noted the various state limits on the amount that a tenant can be charged as a security deposit.

Deadlines for Security Deposit Returns: Details are provided under this listing regarding the time limits imposed by each state for the return of a tenant's security deposit.

Interest Required on Security Deposits: This listing provides each state's requirements regarding whether a landlord must provide interest to the tenant for the holding period of the tenant's security deposit.

Separate Account Required for Security Deposits: This listing specifies whether a landlord is required to keep tenant security deposits in a separate bank account.

Q22. Discuss about the roles and responsibilities of a property manager?

Ans: the property manager roles and responsibilities include the following:

- collection of rent against receipt;
- getting essential repairs done on behalf of the landowner;
- inspection of the premises from time to time;
- giving notice to the tenant
- help in the resolution of disputes among tenants
- any other matters relating to tenancy.

Q23. What sort of notice landlord or the property manager can provide to a tenant?

Ans: Some types of notice are as follows:

- proper maintenance of the premise
- delay in payment of rent
- Revision of rent
- take possession of premises
- renewal of tenancy

Q24. Can a landlord or tenant withhold essential service or supplies?

Ans: No, the landlord or tenant cannot withhold essential service or supplies. If it is done, the rent authority shall conduct an inquiry and resolve it as soon as possible.

Q25. Discuss about the Compensation in case of non-Vacancy?

Ans: Under the Act, A landowner is entitled to pay twice the monthly rent for two months and thereafter four times the monthly rent as per section 22.

Q26. Describe the payment of rent during eviction proceedings?

Ans: As per the Act, the landlord may apply to the Rent Court to direct the tenant to pay the rent to the landlord at any stage of proceedings. And the Rent Court may order the tenant to make such payment and all other charges due from the tenant along with penalty.

Q27. Describe the Provision regarding notice of giving up possession by the tenant?

Ans: The tenant who owns any premises to which this Act applies shall observe all the terms and conditions of the tenancy agreement and shall be entitled to the benefits.

Q28. Discuss the powers of rent tribunal/Rent court under the act?

Ans: Some of the powers of the rent tribunal as mentioned under the act are as follows:

- summoning and enforcing the attendance of any person;
- requiring the discovery and production of documents;
- issuing commissions for the examination of the witnesses or documents;
- issuing commission for local investigation;
- receiving evidence on affidavits;
- dismissing an application or appeal for default or deciding it ex-parte;

- setting aside any order of dismissal of any application or appeal for default or any other order passed by it ex-parte;
- execution of its order and decisions under this Act without reference to any civil court;
- reviewing its orders and decisions;
- any other matter which may be prescribed.

CHAPTER 15

MAHARASHTRA CO-OPERATIVE SOCIETIES ACT

A co-operative housing society is a membership-based legal entity made of one or more residential buildings. You become a member by buying shares in the housing co-operative. In return, as a member, you get the right to occupy a housing unit in the society, be it an apartment or a house. A commonly accepted definition states that in a housing co-operative, the members "pursue the same cause of meeting the common need of housing or its improvement based on mutual assistance." To elaborate, it is a democratically governed enterprise that entails voluntary management, shared expenses and community living. To borrow from Alexander Dumas' The Three Musketeers – One for all, and all for one – is the motto of a co-operative

1. **What are the characteristics of a housing society?**

    - Open to all: Regardless of your gender, caste, social status, political or religious beliefs, you are welcome to join a co-operative housing society.

    - Voluntary organizations: Housing societies are voluntary in their functioning, based on the idea of self-help and self-reliance.

    - Democratic Ownership: Co-operatives are by the people, for the people, of the people. Office bearers/

representatives are chosen through a fair process of election.

- Self-regulation: Co-operative housing societies are operated and governed by members, thus are truly autonomous and independent in all aspects.

- Training and information: Co-operatives train and educate members concerning management, legal compliance, and benefits of communal living so that they can perform their parts effectively.

- Mutual help: By means of various local, national and international structures and paradigms, co-operatives enable members to follow best practices and help them create better living conditions.

- Concern for members: Welfare, convenience and prosperity of every member is the priority of a co-operative without self-interest and power plays within its functioning.

- Financial contribution: Each member contributes equally towards common properties and maintenance.

- Limited liability: Expenses are shared equally in maintenance and to the extent of the contribution made by each member

- Legal entity: A registered co-operative is a legal entity subject to local, national laws

2. **What are the reasons behind the formation of a Society?**

   Important reasons to form a housing society are as under:

   1. It helps to take conveyance from the owner/Promoter (Builder) according to the provisions of the "Ownership

Flats Act" and the Rules made thereunder, of the right, title and interest, in the land with building/buildings thereon as described in the application for registration of the Society;

2. To manage, maintain and administer the property of the society;

3. If the society is formed, it can raise funds;

4. To undertake and provide, for on its account or jointly with cooperative institution, social-cultural or re-creative activities;

5. To do all things necessary or expedient for the attainment of the objects of the society, as specified in the bye-laws.

3. **How to register the society and which documents required for it?**

After taking possession by the holder, it is required to apply for co-operative society within 4 months. It is mandatory according to the provisions of the "Maharashtra Ownership Flat Act 1963" (rule 10 and 8 of the 1964 act).

Opening a new bank account in the name of society is mandatory. Also, the chief promoter should be appointed during the primary meeting of the members of the society. A builder is mostly appointed as a chief promoter, but if he is not ready to become a chief promoter, any member (from the gala holder) can be appointed or selected as a chief promoter.

Following are the documents that are to be submitted for acquiring permission for opening a bank account:

- Application for opening the bank account by reserving the name of the proposed society in the prescribed format. (On adhesive court fee stamp of Rs.2/-)

- Copy of the minutes of the primary meeting (in the prescribed format)
- Photocopy of the sale deed/development agreement executed between the original owner of the land and builder promoter.
- Photocopy of the 7/12 extract or the property registered card.
- Photocopy of a power of attorney is given to the builder, promoter by the original owner.
- Copy of the order from competent office under Urban Land Ceiling Act 1976.
- Detailed scheme of the proposed society and its nature
- List of the proposed members.

It is necessary to submit the proposal for official registration within three months of the date of getting permission for an opening bank account by reserving the name of the proposed society for registration. If it was not possible to submit the registration proposal within the prescribed time limit for some inevitable reasons, then it is necessary to apply for an extension of the time limit for submitting the proposal of registration by the Chief Promoter.

In case of registration, the chief promoter should have to submit the following documents:

1. Application for registration in the prescribed format under rule 4(1) of the Maharashtra Co-operative Societies Rules 1961-Form A (Annexure A)

    If the number of galas mentioned in the application submitted for registration is more than 10, the inclusion of promoter members is needed for 60 per cent galas out of the total galas built or built in the said application. Otherwise, by preserving such a proposal as immature, it is denied for registration. 60 per cent members out of the total members included in the application for registration must have to sign by their name. 10 members of the different families (Definition of the family) includes mother, father, son, husband, wife, unmarried daughter). Similarly, a minimum of 10 members should be residence in the jurisdiction of the society. As per the government's prevalent policy, even less than 10 member's society can be formed. However, in such proposals, the carpet area of each gala should not be more than 700 sq. ft. Similarly, it is also necessary to ensure that the entire F.S.I will be available as per the rules of prevalent constructions, and there is no possibility of additional construction work.

2. Form-B: Information of proposed society (In prescribed format)

3. Form-C: Information of Promoter Members

4. Form-D: Accounts statement (In prescribed format)

5. Detailed scheme of the proposed societies and their nature.

6. Balance statement of saving accounts in the Pune District Central Co-operative Bank (Share Capital of Rs.500 and in addition Admission fee of Rs.100/- of each promoter member and its total amount)

7. Original challan of payment of Rs.25,00/- as a co-operative housing societies registration fee paid in the Government Treasury.

8. A photocopy of the sale deed or Development agreement executed between the original land owner and builder/promoters.

9. Photocopy of the 7/12 extract or property registration card.

10. Photocopy of the Power of Attorney given to the builder promoters by the original landlord.

11. Photocopy of the NOC from the Charity Commissioner if the land is of Public Trust.

12. A photocopy of the land search report or title certificate from the advocate.

13. Photocopy of the order issued by the competent officer under the Urban Land Ceiling Act.

14. True copy of the construction layout approved by the Municipal Corporation.

15. Photocopy of the permission for commencing construction or of a completion certificate issued by the Municipal Corporation.

16. Architect certificate endorsing the construction of the building of the proposed society.

17. Minimum 10 persons affidavit on the stamp paper of Rs.20 (individual) regarding they are residing in the jurisdiction of the society and there is no residential house, an open plot in their name or in the name of the other persons in the family depend on them in the jurisdiction of the society. (Affidavit should be made before the competent officer).

18. Guarantee letter of the Chief Promoter on the stamp paper of Rs.20/- in the prescribed format registered before the competent officer.

19. Guarantee letter of the builder promoters on the stamp paper of Rs.20/- in the prescribed format 'Z' registered before the competent officer and in accordance with that information in A B C D Table.

Table A: number of gala sale, name to whom it sale, area of the gala, and price.

Table B: number of gala not sold and its area.

Table C: Name of the person to whom the gala was sold and the total amount received from him.

Table D: Details of the expenditure, name of the person to whom the gala was sold, amount of the share capital, amount of the admission fee and price of the gala.

20. A photocopy of the registered agreement executed between the builder promoters and gala holder.

21. A photocopy of the receipt of the payment made in respect of the registration fee of the gala and stamp duty of the promoter members mentioned in the application made for registration.

22. The signature of the minimum 10 promoter members at the end of model bye-laws no 175 is necessary.

4. **Who is a Member?**

   Member is a person who had joined in the application to register their cooperative residential society, which was subsequently registered or a person who was later admitted to society's membership after registration.

5. **What action to be taken if the society has denied membership of the Co-operative Housing Society and has not conveyed the decision regarding membership?**

   The co-operative housing society has not received any decision regarding its membership within 3 months from the date of receiving a membership application, then forwarding an application to the Dy/Asstt/ Registrar of the concerned Housing Society, the applicant can demand the

Deemed Membership. The Registrar may pass legitimate order in regards to the membership by taking an appeal of the applicant and member.

6. **Does a Nominal Member have any rights as a member of the Society?**

   No, it has no rights.

7. **Within how many days does the Secretary have to communicate the Committee's decision to the resigning Associate member?**

   Within 15 days, the secretary has to communicate such a decision to the committee regarding the resigning of the associate member. In case of the resignation is rejected, then the reasons for the same should be recorded in the minutes. And if the resignation is not granted within the specified period, then the same is deemed accepted.

8. **What is the limit of the number of members in a Society?**

   It depends upon the number of flats in the building. The Number of members is selected according to the number of flats.

9. **Can a member be expelled?**

   Yes, a member can be expelled on the following grounds:
   - Has persistently failed to pay the charges due to
   - the society
   - Has wilfully deceived the society by giving false
   - information.
   - Has used his flat for immoral purposes or
   - misused it for illegal purposes habitually

- Has been in the habit of committing breaches of any of the provisions of society's by-laws, which are serious in the Committee's opinion.

- Has furnished false information or omitted to furnish the material information to the Registering Authority at the time of registration of the Society.

- Is classified as a Non-Active member who does not attend at least one meeting of the general body in next five years from the date of classification as Non-Active member with the intimation to such member and Registrar

10. **Is there any difference in procedure in case the land on which the Society is situated is given by Government/ CIDCO/MHADA or any other authority?**

In case the society has been given land by the Government/ CIDCO/ MHADA or any other authority for constructing houses thereon, then notwithstanding anything contained in the bye-laws, admission of a person to membership of the Society, direct or as a result of the transfer of shares and interest of the existing member in the capital/property of the Society, shall be subject to the approval of the concerned competent authorities such as collector of the District.

11. **What are the circumstances under which a person ceases to be a member of society?**

The person shall cease to be a member of the Society in the following circumstances:

i. On his resignation from membership of the Society having been accepted by the Committee.

ii. On transfer of all his shares and interest in the capital/ property of the Society.

iii. On his death.

iv. On his expulsion from the membership of the Society.

v. On being adjudged as an insolvent or legally disabled from continuing as a member.

vi. If the member's whereabouts is not known for continuous seven years and if his shares and interest in the property/capital of the Society are not claimed by anybody else.

vii. On the cessation of right/title and interest as a member in the property of the Society by way of legal attachment or sale.

viii. The committee shall take further action in the matter as indicated in Bye-law No. 61.

12. **What are the provisions regarding membership in the Co-operative Housing Society?**

Eligibility for membership in co-operative Housing Societies is mentioned in section 22(1). Accordingly, any person who is eligible for executing contract under Indian Contract Act 1872, Membership of the Co-operative Housing Society can get to any firm, company or society constituted by law or the registered under societies registration Act 1960 or society, registered under Co-operation law, State Government as Central Government, Local Authority Public Trust. However, ownership rights as a flat owner or gala owner of the Housing societies should have to be acquired by legal documents. Also, the following conditions should have to be fulfilled for the membership under rule 19 of the Co-operative law.

1. It is necessary to make an application for membership in prescribed documents format with prescribed

documents under bye-laws and co-operation Act for taking membership of the society.

2. It is necessary to approve the membership application first by the managing committee and by the general body meeting.

3. Necessary to have eligibility under law, rues bye-laws

4. It is necessary to attached resolution giving powers with an application of membership by company, firm, trust local authorities etc., other than the person.

13. **What are the Transfer Fees?**

Transfer Fees is the sum of money payable by a transferor to the Society for the transfer of his shares along with occupancy right as provided under the Bye-law No. 38(e)(vii). The term Transfer Fees is defined under the Bye-law No. 3(xxvi) of the Model Bye-laws of the Society.

14. **What is the procedure to be followed for the disposal of applications received for the transfer of shares?**

On receipt of notice of transfer of shares, the Secretary of the Society shall place the same before the meeting of the Committee, held next after the receipt of the notice, pointing out whether the member is prima-facia eligible to transfer his shares and interest in the capital/property of the Society, in view of the provisions of Section 29(2)(a) of the Act.

In the event of ineligibility (in view of the provisions of section 29(2) (a) & (b) of the act) of the member to transfer his shares and interest in the capital/property of the Society, the Committee shall direct the Secretary of the Society to inform the member accordingly within 8 days of the decision of the Committee. "No Objection Certificate" of the Society is not required to transfer the shares and interest of the transferor to the transferee.

However, if the transferor or transferee requires such a certificate, he shall apply to the Society and the Committee of the Society may consider such application on merit within one month.

15. **Can society make its bye-laws?**

Society can make its bye-law. The only condition is that they should not be against the Indian Constitution and "Maharashtra Co-operative Societies Rules, 1961".

16. **What are the functions of the first general meeting of a society?**

At the first general meeting of the society, the following business shall be transacted:

1. Election of a President for the meeting,

2. Admission of new members (other than the promoters) who have applied for membership in the society.

3. Receiving and approving the statement of accounts, as prepared by the Chief Promoter of the Society, up to 14 days before the date of the first general meeting of the Society.

4. Constitution of a Provisional Committee until regular elections are held under the bye-laws of the society. The Provisional Committee shall have the same powers and functions as the committee elected as per the bye-laws.

5. Fixing the limit up to which funds may be borrowed.

6. Authorizing the Committee to secure conveyance of the right, title and interest in the property, in the name of the Society, from the Promoter (Builder).

7. Appoint internal auditor of the Society for the year, if necessary and fix his remuneration.

8. Authorize one of the members of the Provisional Committee to call the first meeting of the Provisional Committee.

9. Consider affiliation of the society as a member of the Housing Federation of the District and other institutions mentioned in the bye-law No. 6.

10. Consider any other matter to be brought before the meeting with the permission of the Chair, except those requiring proper notice.

(ALSO, FOLLOWINGS ARE APPLICABLE FOR PLOT-PURCHASED TYPE SOCIETY)

1. To review and approve the report of the Chief Promoter of the Society regarding the work is done and proposed to be done concerning the financial and physical aspects of the scheme of construction.

2. To confirm the agreement for the purchase of the plot/building for the society entered into by the Chief Promoter of the society with the vendors.

3. To approve the site plan and the scheme of construction.

4. To confirm the appointment of the architect of the society made by the Chief Promoter of the society or to appoint an architect if no such appointment is made by the Chief Promoter of the Society or to appoint a new architect in place of the one already appointed.

17. What is the composition of the charges of the Society?

The contribution collected from the members of the society towards outgoings and the establishment of its funds referred to in the by-laws is termed as 'charges'. The charges to be collected may be concerning the following:

1. Property taxes
2. Water Charges
3. Common Electricity Charges
4. Contribution to Repairs and Maintenance Fund
5. Expenses on repairs and maintenance of the lifts of the Society, including charges for the running the lift
6. Contribution to the Sinking Fund
7. Service charges
8. Car Parking Charges
9. Interest on the defaulted charges
10. Repayment of the instalment of the Loan and Interest
11. Non-occupancy Charges
12. Insurance Charges
13. Lease Rent
14. Non-Agricultural Tax
15. Any Other Charges

18. What do you mean by a Sinking Fund?

The Sinking Fund at the rate decided at the meeting of the general body, subject to the minimum of 0.25 per cent per annum of the construction cost of each flat incurred during the construction of the building of the society and certified by the Architect, excluding the proportionate cost of the land

19. **What should the Reserve fund of the society comprise of?**

    The Reserve Fund of the society shall comprise of —

    1. the amounts carried to the said fund, from year to year, out of the net profit of that year, subject to the provisions of Section 66 (1) and (2) of the Act;

    2. all entrance fees received by the society from its members;

    3. all transfer fees received by the society from its members on transfers of the shares, along with the occupancy rights;

    4. all premium received by the society from its members on transfers of their interest in the capital or property of the society;

    5. all donations received by the society, except those received by it for a specific purpose.

20. **What is the advantage of the registration of a Society?**

    The registration of a Society renders it to be a body corporate by the name under which it is registered, with perpetual succession and a common seal and with power to acquire, hold and dispose of the property, to enter into contracts and other legal proceedings and do all such things as are necessary for the purpose for which it is constituted.

21. **By whose signature is the bank account of the society operated?**

    The bank account of the society is operated by the joint signature of Secretary, Chairman, and Treasurer Resolution is passed in that respect in the Managing Committee.

22. **Which files of documents are necessary to keep by society?**

The following files of documents are necessary to keep by the society:

1. All types of the membership application.
2. Transfer of membership application.
3. Application of resignations of the member.
4. Application in respect of expelling from membership.
5. Nomination application (correspondence with member —member wise)
6. Correspondence with Dy./Additional Registrar.
7. Correspondence with various machinery (water, electricity etc.)
8. Document regarding property conveyance.
9. Correspondence regarding repairing /Tenders, bills etc.,
10. Application and correspondence regarding the transfer of Flats.
11. Correspondence regarding allotment of flat.
12. Correspondence regarding allotment of parking place.
13. Vouchers.
14. Counter file of the bank's challan.
15. Counter file of the cheque and share certificates.
16. Correspondence regarding issuing of duplicates share certificates.
17. Registration Certificate with Dy./Asst. Registrar regarding amendment in the bye-laws.

18. Counter file of the carbon copy in the receipt book.
19. Copy of the bill issued to the members.
20. Correspondence in respect of the loan if taken.
21. General Agenda of the society.
22. Annual working report of the managing committee.
23. Audit report.
24. Rectification report of the audit and correspondence in that regard.
25. All types of agenda / Notices.
26. All Record of the election as per election rules.
27. Judicial claims filed by the society or against society and its papers.

23. Can a society charge for visitor parking?

The society can decide by moving a resolution in the general body meeting and by considering the number of visitors, facilities etc., for e.g. In the premises of society, people are coming continuously for professional work therefore, it would be proper to take decision by the society not to levy such charges. However, in this regard, the housing society can decide according to circumstances, but considering the members' convenience and the general body meeting's approval will be necessary for this as a complaint in this regard can be filed in the co-operative court.

24. What action can the managing Committee of the Co-operative Housing Society take against the members to recover dues?

First of all, notice must be issued by the society to the defaulter member. Then, if the member is still defaulting, by taking action under section 101 of the Maharashtra Co-operative Societies Act 1960 and obtaining a recovery certificate, action can be taken against such members.

25. What is the procedure for filing a recovery case under section 101?

Under section 101 of the co-operation law and rule 86 A to 86 F made there, the documents and procedure are prescribed. In short, it is as under.

1. Society must have issue 2 notices of one month period and final notice after resolution of 15 days period, i.e. a total of 3 notices to the member.

2. If the dues amount is not paid even after this notice, resolution of action under section 101should has been the move in should have to move in the managing committee meeting. Thereafter final notice of 15 days should be given to the defaulter member.

3. If the dues amount was not paid even after the final notice, an application issue should have to be submitted to Dy/Asstt. Registrar under section 101. The format V or it is given in the rules under Co-operation law and such documents are available with Housing Federation.

4. While submitting the said case, a Challan of the per cent up to one lakh and above that one to two per cent should be paid in the government Treasury/ Reserve Bank. The said amount can be paid in the government treasury by purchasing stamp paper. The limit up to Rs. 10,000/- is prescribed for stamp Paper. This assessment is being made in limitation of maximum Rs10,000/-, In addition Rd. 500/- (enquiry fee should have to be paid in the

following head in the Reserve Bank of India for the case under section 101/-.

26. **Can a Co-operative housing society stop the water supply of the defaulter members?**

The Society cannot stop the water supply of defaulter member.

27. **Is it expected that a member of the ground floor also has to contribute to expenses incurred on the lift? And at what rate it has to be charged?**

Yes, there is a provision that all members should share the contribution of expenses on the lift in equal proportion. Exception of ground-floor members has not been made in this similarly; Since the expenditure incurred charging of the lift of nature of changing lift, machinery is like capital expenditure. It has been charged on all members, including the ground floor, at the rate of per sq. ft area of the flats/galas.

28. **What complaints can be made to the Co-operative Court?**

Complaints can be made to the Co-operative Court relating to disputes between the members and/or the members of the Society, which fall under Section 91 of the MCS Act, 1960 such as disputes about :

1. Resolutions of the Managing Committee and General Body;

2. The elections of the Managing Committee, except the rejection of nominations, as provided under Section 152-A of the MCS Act, 1960;

3. Repairs, including major repairs internal repairs, leakages;

4. Parking;

5. Allotment of Flats;

6. Escalation of construction cost;

7. Appointment of Developer/Contractor, Architect;

8. Unequal water-supply;

9. Excess recovery of dues from the members;

10. Any other, like disputes which fall within the jurisdiction of the Co-operative Court.

29. **Is the sanction of the general body meeting for the re-development of the Society necessary?**

   Yes, the quorum of ¾ of the total number of members in the general body meeting will move resolution regarding re-development. Similarly, to pass such a resolution by approving the re-development scheme by more than ¾ members of the members present in this meeting is obligatory. The government has circulated directives in this regard under section 79 (AB).

30. **What is the provision if the quorum of the special general body meeting is not completed for re-development?**

   In a situation where the quorum *(¾ of the total member) for the special general body meeting called for the re-development is not completed then the meeting shall be postponed for 8 days.*

   However, if the quorum was not able to complete in the postponed meeting, then the meeting shall be cancelled.

31. **To whom is the ownership of open space lie in the Housing Society?**

   All the ownership of the open spaces of co-operative housing society rests with the society. No private person can own such open spaces.

32. **What are the objectives of conveyance?**

   The objectives of conveyance are:

   - The main objective of conveyance is to become a lawful owner of the property because all the property is recognised from its title documents.
   - It indicates that a person has a free and marketable title. Only when the person has a free and marketable title over the property, he/she can sell that particular property.

33. **Which papers should be collected from the builder?**

   Following papers are collected from the builder.

   1. Development agreement.
   2. Death certificate of the deceased landowner.
   3. Partnership agreement between partners.
   4. Evidence of registering partnership agreement.
   5. Conveyance agreement with the builder.
   6. Paper agreement (with the previous owner and with the builder.)
   7. A will, copy of the authorized will(If the legal heir signed the Development Agreement)

34. **Suppose if a builder dies then what steps should be taken for getting Conveyance?**

If the builder dies then the notice regarding the conveyance should be given to the land owner. After that new 7/12 extract or property card should be made. Then such notice should be issued to everyone whose name appears on 7/12 or property card.

35. **When 10 years have lapsed in registration of the society, even when the conveyance has not taken place and the builder is not ready to make conveyance, What should be done in such a situation?**

In such a situation, after 12 years which is from the date of taking forceful possession, the society can claim themselves as the owner. But the order of the court is required for the same. Also, such societies should submit the evidence. The order of the court could be recognised as Deemed Conveyance. In the end, Stamp Duty should be paid.

CHAPTER 16

EASEMENT ACT

An easement is a right that the property owner has to compel another property owner to allow something to be done or refrain from doing something on the servient element to benefit the dominant tenement. For example – the right of way, right to light, right to air etc.

An easement right is practically similar to an advantage, denying which the owner of one apartment has a privilege to appreciate with respect to that apartment in or over the apartment of someone else, on account of which the last is obliged to experience the ill effects of accomplishing something on his apartment for the benefit of the previous.

Naturally, a property owner achieves the option to proceed, the option to air or option to light, the option to assemble, the privilege to the continuous water stream. All these are known as instances of a property owner's easement rights. The Indian Easement Act says that if an person has delighted in these throughout some undefined time frame, they have a substantial right with no limitation, nearly like it were an advantage.

Q1. What do you understand by 'Easement'? Discuss main characteristics of the right of easement. In what ways easements can be acquired?

Ans.

Definition of Easement. – An "Easement" has been defined in Section 4 of the Indian Easement Act, as follows:

"An easement is a correct which the owner or occupier of certain land has, accordingly, for the useful pleasure in that land, to do and keep on accomplishing something, or to forestall and keep on forestalling something being done, in or upon, or in regard of certain different terrains not his own."

Characteristics of Rights of Easement

1. It is Incorporeal – An Easement is an incorporeal thing whereas the land upon which it is imposed is a corporeal thing. Easements have been described as "rather a fringe to property than the property itself and are not capable in an exact sense of being possessed."

2. The right of easement is a right attached to the ownership of land. The words "as such" used in Section 4 are significant in this connection. They connote that the right of easement is a right enjoyed by a person in his capacity as owner or occupier of certain land. An easement does not exist in gross or independently of the ownership or occupation of some land. If one has no land, he may have only a personal right called a right in gross but not an easement right. A person's rights independently of his being the owner or occupier of some land do not constitute easements. An easement is appended to the land for the useful delight which it is made and goes for it. It isn't the individual right of the or occupier of land to which it is attached. One who is not the owner of the dominant heritage nor is in occupation thereof cannot exercise the right of easement.

In *AIR 1981 Pat. 133*, it was observed that An Easement is always appurtenant to dominant land and inseparably attached to it and cannot be severed from it. There can be no easement without a dominant tenement and a servient tenement.

Similarly, in AIR 1955 A.P. 199, an easement is a right or interest in immovable property. Its benefits and burdens pass to every person into whose occupation the dominant and servient tenements respectively come.

3. The Right of easement essentially thinks about two types of land. One is for the helpful pleasure wherein the privilege of advantage exists and the other on which the liability is imposed. The formers are called "dominant heritage" and the latter "servient heritage". As regards the owner of the dominant heritage, an easement involves an enhancement of his ordinary rights and as regards the owner of "servient heritage", it involves a corresponding diminution in his ordinary eights.

These terms have been defined in Section 4 of the Easements Act, as follows

The land for the beneficial enjoyment of which the right exists is called the dominant heritage, and owner or occupier thereof the dominant owner; the land on which the liability is imposed is called the servient heritage, and the owner or occupier thereof the servient owner.

Q2. What is Dominant owner and Servient owner?

Ans: Dominant heritage and dominant owner. The land for the beneficial enjoyment of Easement's right exists called dominant heritage and the owner or occupier thereof the dominant owner. There can be no easement in gross and the establishment of Easements is prevailing legacy or apartment as it is known in English Law. A public road or highway is never a right of Easement. The easement is a privilege of the Dominant owner or occupier. The public local area or a segment of general society or part of a local area can have no privilege of Easement. An Easement is consistently appurtenant to the predominant apartment and is indivisibly appended to it and can't be cut off from it and made a privilege in gross.

Servient heritage and servient owner. – The land upon which the liability of an easement is imposed is called servient heritage or servient tenement and the owner thereof servient owner. It must be land or other corporeal property, but it can, in no case, be incorporeal hereditaments though in English Law, it is possible in certain cases. Nonetheless, no close to home commitment is forced on the servient owner. Servient owner can't demand the continuation of Easements as they are implied distinctly for the Dominant owner.

Right of easement exists only for the beneficial enjoyment of the dominant tenement. It is not something apart from the dominant tenement and that is why Section 6 of the Transfer of Property Act provides that the right of the easement cannot be transferred apart from the dominant tenement.

In *AIR 1988 Kerala 298,* it was observed that characteristics essential to an easement are that there must be a dominant and servient tenement, the easement must accommodate the dominant tenement the right of the easement must be possessed for the beneficial enjoyment of dominant tenement, dominant and Servient owners must be different persons. The right should entitle the dominant owner to do and continue to do something or prevent and continue to prevent something being done in or upon or in respect of the servient tenement and must be of a well-defined character capable of forming the subject matter of a grant.

Q3. Distinguish between (i) an easement and a license, (ii) an easement and a customary right and (iii) an easement and a natural right.

Ans:

I. **An Easement and a Licence.** –

   i. An easement is a right appertaining to property while a licence is only a personal right.

   ii. An easement is a right against an individual but known to the whole world. It is enforceable by all against all into whose hands the servient and dominant properties go. License is only personal and known to individual only.

   iii. An easement can be assigned with the property to which it is annexed, but a licence cannot be assigned at all except where it is a licence to attend a place of public entertainment.

   iv. An easement is not revocable at the will of the grantor while a licence is so revocable.

   v. A licence is permission traceable to a grant from the licensor, whereas easement is acquired by assertive enjoyment or negative enjoyment, grant or statute.

   vi. An easement may be positive or negative. A licence is invariable of positive character. It is never negative.

II. **Easements and Customary Rights.** – The Indian Easement Act does not deal with Customary rights. The following differences however may be noted:-

   i. A custom may be good though its exercise may have the effect of depriving the owner of the soil of the whole and enjoyment of his property. Right of Easement must not tend to the total deprivation of the rights of the servient owner.

   ii. Where an easement claimed is not a customary right, it needs not be reasonable whereas the custom must always be reasonable.

iii. An Easement, which cannot be prevented, cannot be acquired by prescription. There is no such rule regarding the acquisition of a customary right.

iv. One who relies on custom must prove that it was ancient, continuous, peaceable, reasonable, certain, compulsorily observed, consistent with other customs and not inconsistent with the statute. A customary right's origin is generally to common consent and when fully developed, may be treated as incorporated into a contract by implication. It is not always so with Easements.

III. **Easements and Natural Rights.** – The following distinctions are significant:-

i. Natural rights are inherent in the land, but Easements are created at the will of the owner of the land over which they are to be used. (Goddard on Easements 7th Edition, p. 33).

ii. Natural rights are certain incidents and advantage which Nature provides for the use and enjoyment of a man's property. (Peacock on Easement 2nd Edition p. 24). They are capable of separate existence and can be disposed of separately whereas easements cannot be so dealt with.

iii. Natural rights are rights in rem, that is, enforceable against all who may violate them. The remedy is an action for trespass, whereas infringement of easement is a nuisance.

iv. Easements rights are taken from the ownership of one man and are added to ownership of another. Natural lights are themselves part of the complete rights of ownership, they belong to the ordinary incidents of property and are ipso facto enforceable in law.

v. Easements are only to be created and conferred by the act of man whereas natural rights are incidents of land.

In **AIR 1967 A.P. 81,** it was observed 'Easement are distinct from Natural rights. Natural rights are those rights that constitute the ordinary incidents of a property and wherein a person by under virtue of his ownership of that property while easement denotes right acquired by another person having the effect of restricting these natural rights of owner or property.

Q4. Explain and distinguish between Continuous and Discontinuous Easements.

Ans: According to Section 5, "Easements are either continuous or discontinuous, apparent or non-apparent.

A continuous easement is one whose enjoyment is or may be continued without the act of man.

A discontinuous easement needs the act of man for its enjoyment.

The Distinction between continuous and discontinuous easements. – An easement is a right either

1. to do or continue to do something or
2. prevent or continue to prevent something being done on servient heritage. The former right requires an act of man for its enjoyment and is, therefore, discontinuous. The latter right consists of merely preventing something being done upon the servient heritage, such as an obstruction to light or air received there and did not require any act of man for the enjoyment of the right. It is, therefore, a continuous easement.

A right is annexed to B's house to receive light by the windows without obstruction by his neighbour A. This is a continuous easement. The reason is that its enjoyment is continued without the act of a man. A drain is also a continuous easement. So is the person's right to an uninterrupted flow of a permanent artificial stream to his land.

However, a right of way is a discontinuous easement, for it needs the act of man for its enjoyment.

Q5. Explain and distinguish between Apparent and non-apparent Easement.

Ans: **Distinction Between Apparent and Non-apparent Easement** – According to Section 5 of the Indian Easement Act, "an apparent easement is one the existence of which is shown by some permanent sign which upon careful inspection by a competent person, would be visible to him."

"A non-apparent easement has no such sign."

So, an easement is apparent where its existence is shown by some external permanent mark or sign on servient heritage which is either visible to everyone or to one who cases to look to it. A non-apparent easement has no such signs. A right annexed to 'A's house to prevent 'B' from building on his land is a non-apparent easement. But doors, windows, skylights, drains are apparent easement.

Q6. "Easement rights are restrictions on owner rights."- Discuss.

Ans: Section 7 of the Indian Easements Act reads as under -

Easement restrictive of certain rights. – Easements are restrictions of one or other of the following rights (namely) -

a. **Exclusive rights to enjoy** – The exclusive right of every owner of immovable property (subject to any law for the time being in force) to enjoy and dispose of the same and all products thereof and accession thereto.

b. **Rights to advantages arising from the situation** – The right of every owner of immovable property (subject to any law for the time being in force) to enjoy without disturbance by another, the natural advantages arising from its situation.

Explanation – Land is in its natural condition when it is not excavated and not subjected to artificial pressure. The subjacent and adjacent soil mentioned in this illustration means such soil only as in its natural condition would support the dominant heritage in its natural condition.

Explanation – A natural stream is a stream, whether permanent or intermittent, tidal or tideless, on the surface of land or underground, which flows by the operation of nature only and in a natural and known course. [Section 7]

Right of ownership consists of a bundle of minor or fragmentary rights each right capable of separate enjoyment. The owner's absoluteness in his property consists in his power to dispose of as he please any of these fragmentary rights. Easementary rights consist of (sic) of possession or enjoyment. These rights are carved out of the right of ownership by a restrictive process and are restrictions on the owner's power of full use and enjoyment.

In **AIR 1957 M.P. 44,** it was observed that an easement right is curved out in favour of a dominant heritage and is imposed on servient heritage. In every case, right is exercised by qua owner or occupier of dominant heritage and falls as a burden on the owner or occupier of servient heritage.

Q7. Who are riparian owners? Discuss the rights of riparian owners. Have they any natural right to use water to irrigate their land without diminution of flow of water?

Ans: Riparian **Owners**:- "Riparian" suggests water or river running between the banks, be it salty or fresh; and "Riparian Owners" are owners of the land on the bank of a river or a stream.

i. The right of each owner of land adjoining a characteristic stream, lake and lake to utilize and burn-through its water for drinking, family purposes and watering his steers and sheep and the privilege of each such owner to utilize and devour the water for flooding such land, and for any assembling arrange consequently: given that he doesn't along these lines cause material injury to other like owners.

Natural Rights of a Riparian Owner. – The following are some of the natural rights of a riparian owner. They are the same as in England:-

ii. by the overall law appropriate to running streams, each riparian owner has an option to what exactly might be known as the conventional utilization of water streaming past his property, for example, the sensible utilization of water for his homegrown purposes and for steers. Yet, further he has a privilege to utilize water for some other purposes furnished he doesn't along these lines meddle with the privileges of different owners, regardless of whether above or underneath him. Subject to this condition, he may dam up the stream for his factory or redirect the water for water system. This is the common right. Be that as it may, he has no option to intrude on the normal progression of the stream which can be procured uniquely as an easement.

The riparian owner's right is confined only to the usufruct of the stream which passes through a riparian owner's land. He has no property in the water itself, but he has simply the right to use it.

iii. Every riparian owner of land has a characteristic right that the water of each regular stream which cruises by, through or over his territory in a characterized normal channel will be permitted by different people to stream inside such proprietor's cutoff points interference and without material modification in amount, bearing, power or temperature. He has a comparable right in regard of water of lake or lake adjoining his territory into or out of which normal stream follows.

iv. Every riparian owner can demand that the water coming to him ought not be contaminated or delivered unsuitable for his homegrown use or harmful to his property or dairy cattle.

In **AIR 1954 Pat. 320 (DB)**, it was observed that every riparian owner of the natural stream has a natural right as an incident to the ownership of the soil abutting on the stream, to the benefit and advantage of the water flowing past his land subject however to limitation of not interfering ever to the limitation of not interfering with the quality or quantity of water of the stream to which the lower riparian proprietors are entitled under similar rights.

Q8. Discuss the provisions of the Indian Easement Act regarding the imposition of the easement.

Ans: *Imposition of Easement*: Sections 8 to 11 of the Easement Act deal with the imposition of Easement. The word "impose" in sections of Chapter-II of the Act means creating an easement by a voluntary act of the owners or lessee or any other person having the power to transfer an interest in the servient tenement.

According to Section 8 of the Easement Act, "Anyone in the circumstances may impose an Easement, and to the extent, in and to which he may transfer his interest in heritage on which the liability is to be imposed."

So, section 8 of the Act permits the servient owner to impose an easement on his property.

Then Section 9 of Easement Act says:-

"Subject to provisions of Section 8, a servient owner may impose on the servient heritage any easement that does not lessen the utility of the existing easement. But he cannot without the dominant owner's consent, imposing an easement on the servient heritage that would lessen such utility.

A has, in respect of his house, a right of way over B' Land. B may grant to C, as the owner of a neighbouring farm, the rights to feed his cattle on the grass growing on the way. Provided that A's right to way is not thereby obstructed.

Then Section 10 of Act says, "Subject to provisions of Section 8, a lessor may impose, on the property leased, any easement that does not derogate from the rights of the lessee, as such and a mortgagor may impose, on the property mortgaged, any easement that does not render the security insufficient. But a lessor or mortgagor cannot, without the consent of the lessee or mortgagee, impose any other easement on such property unless it is to take effect on the termination of the lease or the redemption of the mortgage." Section 11 says, "No lessee or other person having a derivative interest may impose on the property held by him as such an easement to take effect after the expiration of his own interest, or in derogation of the right of the lessor or the superior proprietor.

So, the law does not prevent a tenant from granting easement by express or implied grant commensurate with the extent of his interest.

Q9. Who may acquire easement? Can a tenant acquire easement against his landlord?

Ans: An easement may be acquired by the owner of the immovable property for the beneficial enjoyment of which the right is created or, on his behalf, by any person in possession of the same.

One of two or more co-owners of immovable property may, as such, with or without consent of the other or others, acquire an easement for the beneficial enjoyment of such property. No lessee of immovable property can acquire, for the beneficial enjoyment of other immovable property of his own, an easement in or over the property comprised in his lease. [Section 12]

In **AIR 1987 Raj. 169**, it was observed that the owner of the immovable property could acquire an easement for the beneficial enjoyment of a right by any person in possession of the same. The incidence of easement and that of the lost grant are almost the same. Right of easement is also created by grant and grant of such use may be presumed from long use or possession although actual transaction of making such grant could not be discovered.

As easement may be acquired by the owner of immovable property for the beneficial enjoyment of which the right is created, or on his behalf by any person in possession of the same [*Nihal Chand v. Mst. Bhagwan Dei, A.I.R. 1934 All. 527*]. Such an easement shall not, however, be personal to him. If the physical acts of the dominant owner are of such a nature as to entitle him to acquire the right of easement, he is entitled to that right although that he was doing those acts under the belief that he was the owner of the servient heritage. But it would be otherwise if he had asserted and claimed ownership in earlier litigation. [*Shivpyari v. Mst. Sardari, A.I.R. 1966 Raj. 265*].

Acquisition of easement by a tenant against his landlord – Tenant can acquire an easement over the adjoining land belonging to his landlord for the beneficial enjoyment of other immovable property not his own but belonging to someone else which also he happens to occupy for the time being as a tenant. [**A.I.R. 1939 All. 339**]. A tenant cannot acquire an easement by prescription against his landlord. CHIRNS explains the reason for this rule. L.J. in Goyford v. Muffat in the following words:

"The possession of the tenant of the demised close land is in possession of his landlord; and it seems to be an utter violation of the first principle of the relation of landlord and tenant to suppose that the tenant, whose occupation of the close A was the occupation of his landlord, could, by that occupation acquire as an easement over close B also belonging to his landlord."

Q10. An Easement of necessity is a right which owner or occupier of land must of necessity exercise over the land of another for the enjoyment of his own land." – Explain the statement and distinguish between easement of necessity and Quasi easement.

Ans: **Easement of Necessity** – Section 13 of Indian Easement Act says-

Where a one-person transfer or bequeaths immovable property to another-

a. if an easement in other immovable property of the transferor or testator is necessary for enjoying the subject of the transfer or bequest, the transferee or legatee shall be entitled to such easement; or

b. if such an easement is apparent and continuous and necessary for enjoying the said subject as it was enjoyed when the transfer or bequest took effect, the transferee or legatee shall, unless a different intention is expressed or necessarily implied, be entitled, to such easement:

c. if an easement in the subject of the transfer or bequest is necessary for enjoying other immovable property of the transferor or testator the transferor or the legal representative of the testator shall be entitled to such easement; or

d. if such an easement is apparent and continuous and necessary for enjoying the said property as it was enjoyed when the transfer or bequest took effect, the transferor, or the testator's legal representative, shall unless a different intention is expressed or necessarily implied, be entitled to such easement.

Where a partition is made of the joint property of several persons -

e. if an easement over the share of one of them is necessary for enjoying the share of another of them, the latter shall be entitled to such easement; or

f. if such an easement is apparent and continuous and necessary for enjoying the share of latter as it was enjoyed when the partition took effect, he shall, unless a different intention is expressed or necessarily implied, be entitled to such easement.

The easement mentioned in Clauses (a)(c) and (e) of this section is called easements of necessity.

Where immovable property passes by operation of law, the persons from and to whom it so passes are, for this section, to be deemed, respectively, the transferor and transferee."

In *AIR 1984 Orissa 97*, it was observed that Easement of necessity is one which the law creates according to the doctrine of implied grant in a particular case and is one without which the dominant tenement cannot be used at all. Easement of need emerges just whereby an exchange, endowment or segment, a solitary apartment is partitioned into particular and separate tenements. Any of the apartment is arranged to the point that it can't be utilized at all without getting a charge out of an easement over the other such tenement or tenements.

Where one property is served from another property either in possession or ownership, or in both by move, estate, or segment or by activity of law and these two are so moderately arranged that once can't be appreciated without the activity of a specific advantage in or upon or in regard of the other, such advantage is known as the easement of necessity.

An easement of necessity is an easement which under particular circumstances the law creates by nature of the doctrine of implied grant to meet the necessity of a particular case. It is an easement that isn't just important for the sensible delight in the predominant tenement, yet one without which the tenement can't be utilized by any means. Convenience is not the test of easement of necessity. An easement of necessity can be claimed only when there is an absolute necessity for it. Subsequently, a man can't procure an easement of need on the off chance that he has some other methods for admittance to his territory, anyway badly arranged it very well might be, than by ignoring his neighbour's soil.

Easements of quasi Necessity:

The clauses (b), (d) and (f) of Section 13 deal with what are called quasi- easements. These are not exactly easementary rights but are only modes of enjoyment of property that resemble easementary rights in several characteristics. Strictly speaking, these rights are easements before severance because both parts are before severance under common ownership. The modes of enjoyment themselves are converted into easement rights.

Examples of Easement of Quasi Necessity:

i. Right of irrigation,

ii. Rights of lights and air,

iii. Right of path, way and drainage when they are apparent and continuous.

Easement of Necessity and quasi-Necessity Compared:

1. The easement of need is the easement without which the concerned property can't be utilized and delighted in by any means. In any case, the quasi easement is that without which the sensible, agreeable and more helpful utilization of the property would not be possible.

2. The easement of need assumes the vesting of responsibility for tenements initially in a similar individual and the severance of such possession. Earlier joint ownership and unity of possession are fundamental. In easements of semi need, the utilization doesn't begin after severance yet has proceeded even previously. The severance permits it to proceed on the ground that it is sensible to do as such.

3. In easement of need, the reason is supreme need while in the easement of semi need, it is a solitary qualified need.

4. The easement of quasi – necessity relies on whether it is evident, consistent and more advantageous or sensible. However, in the easement of need, nothing is needed to be demonstrated. The easements of need can be asserted regardless of whether easements are non-evident or discontinuous. In any case, easements of quasi necessity can't be so asserted.

Q11. How can prescription acquire a right of the easement? What are the essentials for acquiring such easementary right?

Ans: Acquisition of Easement by Prescription. – Section 15 of the Easements Act provides that where the access and use of light or air to and for any building have been peaceably enjoyed in addition to that, as an easement, without interruption, and for twenty years, and where support from one person's land subjected to artificial pressure or by things affixed thereto as an easement without interruption, and for twenty years, and where a right of way or any other easement has been peaceably and openly enjoyed by any person claiming title thereto, as an easement, and as of right without interruption, and for twenty years, the right to such access and use of light or air, support or another easement shall be absolute.

Each of the said periods of twenty years shall be taken to be a period ending within two years next before the institution of the suit wherein the claim to which such period relates is contested.

Section 15 has been divided into three parts:

Part one deals with the right to the access and use of light or air to and for any building.

Part two deals with the right of support.

Part three deals with general things including the right of way.

Conditions Necessary for Acquisition of Prescriptive Easement-

i. The right claimed must be certain and must be against a specific individual.
ii. Enjoyed independently.
iii. Without any agreement with the owner of servient land or must be non-permissive. It is always hostile and resembles in some respects to claim ownership by adverse possession.
iv. Enjoyment must have been:
   a. peaceful or Nec vi (without violence),
   b. Open or Nec clam (without stealth),
   c. As of right, or necprecario (without permission),
   d. As an easement,
   e. Without interruption,
   f. For twenty years or sixty years (If Government Estate).

The easement of light and support and air need not have been enjoyed openly and as a matter of right but regarding other easementary rights, these are necessary elements.

In *AIR 1971 SC 1878,* it was observed that to establish prescriptive acquisition of right one must prove that he was exercising that right on a property treating it as someone else's.

In *AIR 1986 Kerala 75(79),* it was observed that an easement could become absolute by prescription there must be pre-existing easement which must have been enjoyed by the dominant owner the enjoyment must be peaceful, which must have been as an easement as of right the right must have been openly enjoyed for 20 years without interruption.

Q12. What is the acquisition of an easement by prescription?

Ans: The following are the conditions for the acquisition of easement rights by prescription:

1. The right to possess by the owner or occupier of dominant heritage against the servient heritage. There should be two different pieces of land owned by two different persons for the existent of an easementary right.

2. The right of way and other varieties can be acquired if:

    a. they have been enjoyed

    b. as an easement;

    c. for 20 years; or 30 years (if the right is claimed against the Government);

    d. without interruption by a person claiming title to them;

    e. openly;

    f. peaceably; and

    g. as of right;

Easement privileges of light, air and support can be obtained in the event that they have been serenely delighted in, without interference as an easement for a very long time. The privilege of light, air and support need not be appreciated either transparently or as of right or by an individual asserting title thereto. Such easement can be procured by serene pleasure without its satisfaction as of appropriate for an endorsed period.

According to Section 17 of the Indian Easements Act, none of the following rights can be acquired:

a. a right which would tend to total description of the subject of the right, or the property on which, if the acquisition were made, liability would be imposed;

b. a right to the free passage of light or air to an open space of ground;

c. a right to surface water not flowing in a stream and not permanently collected in a pool, tank or otherwise;

d. a right to underground water not passing in a defined channel.

In ***Het Singh and others v. Aman Singh and others (AIR 1982 All. 968)***, it has been held that under Section 17(a), a right to underground water not passing in a defined channel cannot be acquired by prescription under Section 15.

A right to draw water from a well is a right to underground water. Therefore, the right to irrigate the field from the well situated in another's land cannot be acquired as an easementary right by prescription. The right of easement by prescription cannot become absolute unless the right has been contested in a suit. Thus, a suit for mere injunction is not maintainable when the suit is based on the alleged prescriptive right without a prayer for a declaration that the plaintiff acquired such prescriptive right [***Dr. Ramanatha Gupta v. S. Razaack (AIR 1982 Karn. 314)***].

Q13. Define customary easement and State the essential requisites of a valid custom. Distinguish between a customary easement and customary right. Illustrate.

Ans: Customary Easement:- Section 18 of the Indian Easement Act defines customary easement. It lays down – "An easement may be acquired by virtue of a local custom; such easements are called customary easements. Though custom and easement are rights of a different kind, there undoubtedly can be a custom in a locality under and by virtue of which an individual may become entitled to an easement in respect of his estate situated in a 'locality' custom belongs. The special feature of these easements is that custom affects an individual not as such but only as a member of some community, and it is a usage annexed to a locality."

A customary easement originates in a valid custom, and a custom to be valid must have four essential attributes. It must be (1) immemorial, (2) reasonable, (3) certain and (4) it must have continued without interruption since its immemorial origin.

Immemorial. – A custom to be valid must be ancient. But it does not mean that its antiquity must, in every case, be carried back to a period beyond the memory of men. It will rely on the conditions of each case regarding what antiquity should be set up before the custom can be acknowledged. It should be demonstrated for building up a custom that considering the specific locale's overseeing rule has been by and by for long. It would make extraordinary perplexity if, for each situation, the artifact of a custom should be conveyed back to a period that is past the memory of man. The rule of Indian Law doesn't endorse any time of delight in demonstrating a legitimate custom.

Reasonable. – Reasonableness of a custom ought to be seen concerning its commencement. In the event that a custom is absurd at its beginning, no utilization or duration can make it great. The sensibility of a custom should not be judged in light of an untaught man however by counterfeit legitimate reasons justified by power of law.

Certain. – The custom should be sure in regard of its inclination by and large and in regard of the territory where it is affirmed to acquire and the people it is asserted to influence.

The Distinction between a customary easement and customary rights. – Customary easement and customary right have both their cause in custom and to that degree, they are comparative. A customary right is a public right having a place with no specific individual except for to every one of the individuals who possess a specific territory or have a place with a class of people qualified for the advantage which isn't appurtenant to any land. An easement is certifiably not a public right. It is a private right having a place with some specific individual or people in regard of his or their property. For instance, an option to consume Holi or to have horse races on another's property is a customary right on the grounds that a privilege has a place with general society of a specific spot and not to a specific individual; in addition, it isn't added to land. Then again, a customary easement, for example, as the easement of protection, however dependent on custom, is certainly not a standard right as each proprietor of a house in a specific territory has a right, in regard of his home, that his neighbour will, by opening new windows, not attack his security and the privilege is his private right not imparted to other people.

Q 14.

a. **Explain the expression "right of privacy". State the law relating to the Right of Privacy as an easement. Is the right to undisturbed privacy recognised in this country?**

b. **Can a right of privacy be claimed in the following cases:-**

   i. **In respect of apartments generally occupied and used by males.**

   ii. **By a Christian lad who does not observe Purdah in respect of her private apartments.**

   iii. **In respect of an already overlooked house by the opening of additional apertures.**

   iv. **In respect of a house separated from the other by a narrow public lane.**

Give reasons for your answers.

Ans:

a. **Right of Privacy.** – The phrase 'right of privacy is used in the Indian Case Law to refer to the right which an owner of a house may have under local custom to the seclusion of his inner apartments from the view of his neighbour.

The right to privacy is a customary easement and may be acquired under a local custom under Section 18 of the Easements Act. The Law on the subject has been laid down in this way in English Law "concerning the question of privacy, no doubt, the owner of a house would prefer that a neighbour should not have the right of looking to his windows or yards, but neither this court nor a court of law, will interfere on the mere ground of invasion of privacy; and a party has a right even to open new windows, although he is thereby enabled to overlook his neighbour's premises, and to interfere perhaps with his comfort". The same is the law in India except in the provinces where a right of privacy exists by custom. The right of privacy does not arise from prescription but is a creation of custom.

In **AIR 1988 SC 2024,** it was observed right of privacy was neither pleaded nor proved. If one party opens a window, it is equally open to another party to block them by raising walls. No natural right to privacy inheres in the property owner, which would extend to his obstructing a window opened in his neighbour's buildings.

b. (i) Under Section 18 of the Easements Act, such an easement of privacy can be acquired by virtue of a local custom. In India, there is a difference in respect of this right in different parts of India. In U.P., Gujarat, Bombay, Punjab and not in Madras where the purdah system is observed, the right to respect apartments where ladies reside can only be claimed. In the above case, the house or portion of a house that is not meant to be occupied by females and consequently is not ordinarily excluded from observation will not be protected, e.g., a sitting room.

    ii. A right of privacy is a right that attaches to the property and is not dependant on the owner's religion. (***Abdul Rahman v. D. Emile, 16 I.A. 49***). So if there was a right of privacy in the house, even a Christian lady who does not observe purdah could claim it.

    iii. It depends on the circumstances of each case. Where the defendants opened certain apertures towards the plaintiff's house which was already overlooked by the defendants' house in several places, it was held that there was a substantial and material invasion of the right of privacy as the apertures would permit a person to look on without being observed which would be guarded against from an open space. (29 All.852 Supra).

    iv. The existence of a lane in between would not destroy the right of privacy. In order to establish the right to privacy, it does not matter whether the house in question is on the same side of the street or the opposite side of it. So the right of privacy can be claimed in respect of a house separated from the other by a narrow public lane.

Q.15 What are the reasonable modes in which a dominant owner can exercise his easement? Discuss the main incidents.

Ans: Sections 21 to 31 of the Indian Easements Act deal with the incidents of easements. The sections are reproduced below-

Bar to use unconnected with enjoyment – An easement must not be used for any purpose not connected with the enjoyment of the dominant heritage. [Section 21]

Illustrations

a. A, as the owner of a farm, has the right of way over B's land to Y. Lying Y, A has another farm Z, the beneficial enjoyment of which is not necessary for the beneficial enjoyment of Y. He must not use the easement for the purpose of passing to and from Z.

b. A, as the owner of a certain house, has the right of way to and from it. For the purpose of passing to and from the house, the right may be used, not only by A but by the members of his family, lodgers, servants, workmen, visitors and customers; for this is a purpose connected with the enjoyment of the dominant heritage. If A lets the house, he may use the right to collect the rent and see that the house is kept in repair.

Exercise of easement-Confinement of exercise of easement – The dominant owner must exercise his right in the mode which is at least one route to the servient owner. When the exercise of an easement cannot be a detriment to the dominant owner be confined to a determinate part of the serveint heritage, such exercise shall be so confined at the request of the servient owner. [Section 22]

a. A has the right of way over B's field. A must enter the way at either end and not at any intermediate point.

b. A has a right annexed to his house to cut thatching grass in B's swamp. A when exercising his easement must cut the grass so that the plants may not be destroyed.

Right to alter the mode of enjoyment – Subject to the provisions of Section 22, the dominant owner may, from time to time, alter the mode and place of enjoyment of the easement provided that he does not thereby impose any additional burden on the servient heritage.

Exception – The dominant owner of a right of way cannot vary his line of passage at pleasure, even though he does not thereby impose any additional burden on the servient heritage. [Section 23]

It can easily be inferred from reading sections 23 and 45 of the Indian Easement Act that the enjoyment of the easement can be extinguished only when the place where the easement is enjoyed is permanently altered to impose an extra burden on the service heritage. [*Chaturbhuj v. Ramjeevan, A.I.R. 1976 Raj. 164*].

Right to do acts, to secure enjoyment – The dominant owner entitled, as against the servient owner, to do all acts necessary to secure the full enjoyment of the easement; but such act must be done at such time and in such manner as, without detriment to the dominant owner, to cause the servient owner as little inconvenience as possible; and the dominant owner must repair, as far as practicable the damage (if any) caused by the act to the servient heritage. [Section 24]

Accessory Right – Rights to do acts necessary to secure the full enjoyment of an easement are called accessory rights.

Illustrations

a. A has an easement to lay pipes in B's land to convey water to A's cistern. A may enter and dig the land in order to mend the pipes, but he must restore the surface to its original state.

b. A has an easement of drainage through B's land. The sewer with which the drain communicates is altered. A may enter upon B's land and alter the drain to adapt to the new sewer, provided that he does not thereby impose any additional burden on B's land.

Liability For Expenses Necessary For Preservation of Easement:- The dominant owner must defray the expenses incurred in constructing works or making repairs or doing another act necessary for the use or preservation of an easement. (Section 25)

Servient Owner Not Bound To Do Anything – The servient owner is not bound to do anything for the benefit of the dominant heritage and he is entitled as against the dominant owner to use the servient heritage in any way consistent with the enjoyment of the easement. However, he must not do any act tending to restrict the easement or render its exercise less convenient. (Section 27)

The extent of easement – Concerning the extent of easements and the mode of their enjoyment, the following provisions shall take effect:-

Easement of necessity – An easement of necessity is co-extensive with the necessity as it existed when the easement was imposed.

Other easements – The extent of any other easement and the mode of its enjoyment must be fixed concerning the probable intention of the parties and the purposes for which the right was imposed or acquired.

In the absence of evidence as to such intention and purpose -

a. **Right of way** – A right of way of any kind does not include a right of any other kind;

b. **Right to the light or air acquired by grant** – The extent of the right to the passage of light or air to a certain window, door or other opening imposed by a testamentary or non-testamentary instrument is the quantity of light or air that entered the opening at the time the testator died or the non-testamentary instrument was made;

c. **Prescriptive right to light or air** – he extent of a prescriptive right to the passage of light or air to certain windows, door or other opening is that quantity of light of air which has been accustomed to enter that opening during the whole of the prescriptive period irrespective of the purposes for which it has been used.

d. **Prescriptive right to pollute air and water** – The extent of prescriptive right to pollute air or water is the extent of pollution at the commencement of the period of the user on completion of which the right arose; and

e. **Other prescriptive rights** – The extent of every other prescriptive right and the mode of its enjoyment must be determined by the accustomed user of the right. [Section 28]

Sections 22, 24 and 28 seem to embody the rule that while the claimant of the easementary right should have full protection in the enjoyment of his right; there should be an adjustment with the servient owner's rights the least inconvenience be caused to the latter. [*Ram Narain v. Gangadhar, A.I.R. 1975 All. 259*].

The increase of easements – The dominant owner cannot merely alter or add to the dominant heritage but substantially increase an easement.

Where an easement has been granted or bequeathed so that its extent shall be proportionate to the extent of the dominant heritage, if the dominant heritage is increased, by alluvion, the easement is proportionately increased. If the dominant heritage is diminished by diluvion, the easement is proportionately diminished.

Save as aforesaid, no easement is affected by any change in the extent of the dominant or the servient heritage. [Section 29]

Partition of Dominant Heritage: – Section 30 of the Act says that where a dominant heritage is divided between two or more persons, the easement becomes annexed to each of the shares but not to increase substantially the burden of the servient heritage.

Provided that such annexation is consistent with the terms of the instrument, decree or revenue proceedings (if any) under which the division was made and in case of prescriptive rights with the user during the prescriptive period.

Obstruction in case of Excessive User: – Section 31 says in case of an excessive user of an easement, the servient owner may without prejudice to any other remedies to which he may be entitled obstruct the user, but only on the servient heritage.

Provided that such use cannot be otherwise when obstruction would interfere with the lawful enjoyment.

Q16. What is an accessory easement?

Ans: Accessory Easement – Right to do acts necessary to secure the full enjoyment of an easement is called accessory rights. [Section 24]

A dominant owner is entitled to the full enjoyment of his right of the easement, and if to secure its full enjoyment the doing of certain other secondary acts is necessary, he is naturally and by a presumption of law, entitled to do all those acts also. A right to do such acts is called an accessory right and is incidental to the right of easement. But the acts must be done in such a manner and at such a time as to cause the servient owner as little inconvenience as possible, but without any prejudicial effect on the dominant owner's right.

A, as the owner of a certain house, has the right of way over B's land. The way is out of repair. A may enter on B's land and repair the way, but then it must be so done to cause the servient owner as little inconvenience as possible, the dominant owner must repair the damage caused thereby to the servient heritage.

Accessory easement confers certain auxiliary rights upon the dominant owner. The dominant owner is authorised to perform all such acts on the servient tenement as are necessary for the proper exercise of his easement. However, in performing such acts, if the dominant owner causes any damage to the servient tenement, he must make good this damage and restore the servient tenement to its original condition as far as possible.

Accessory rights are sometimes called "accessory easement" or "secondary easement" and are quite distinct from "subordinate easement" mentioned in Section 9.

Q17. What does amount to a disturbance of an easement?

Ans: Section 32 of the Indian Easement Act provides:-

"The owner or occupier of the dominant heritage is entitled to enjoy the easement without disturbance by any other person."

Illustration 'A' as the owner of a house has the right of way over B's land. C unlawfully enters on B's land and obstructs 'A' in his right of way. A may sue C for compensation, not for the entry but the obstruction.

Disturbance – Meaning: Any act which tends to interfere with or obstruct or inconvenience or diminish the enjoyment of the right of the dominant owner either by servient owner or by any other person the dominant owner is said to be disturbed and has right of suit against obstructing party. The disturbance is a word possessing a special legal significance in English Law. "Gale" in his commentary on Easement has said, "It is not every interference with the full enjoyment of an easement that amounts in law to a disturbance; there must be some sensible abridgement of the enjoyment of the tenement to which it is attached, although there does not need to be total obstruction of the easement. The injury complained of must be substantial in ordinary apprehension of mankind and not arising from the caprice or peculiar physical constitution of the party aggrieved." Whether a particular act causes disturbance of right of easement is a question of fact to be determined in each case concerning the nature of the act, the nature of easement and the circumstances connected with the enjoyment of such easement, and the doing of such act.

In ***Narsoo v. Madan Lal, AIR 1975 M.P. 185***, it was observed that it is no doubt true that u/s 32, the owner or occupier of the dominant heritage, is entitled to enjoy the easement without disturbance by any other person. But before Section 32 is invoked, it is necessary to determine as to what extent of the right of the easement acquired by the owner or occupier of dominant heritage. If he had acquired or if he could acquire legally only the right to use water collected in the pool or the tank and under the law could not acquire a right over the free flow of surface water, it cannot be said that any disturbance is caused by anyone in the enjoyment of the easement by impounding the surface water before it reached the pool or the tank or by diverting it.

Q18. Discuss what constitutes and what does not constitute a disturbance of an easement of light under the Indian Easement Act.

Ans: A person complaining of disturbance of his right of the easement has to succeed in the suit, show not only that there has been a disturbance of an easement or any right accessory thereto, but also to prove that the disturbance has resulted in substantial damage to him.

It is further clear from explanation II of Section 33 of the Act that no damage would be substantial in the case of right of free passage of light through the opening of a house, unless:-

1. It is likely to injure the plaintiff by affecting the evidence of the easement by materially diminishing the value of dominant heritage.

2. It interferes with the physical comfort of the plaintiff; or

3. Prevents him from carrying on his accustomed business in the dominant heritage as beneficially as he had done previous to the institution of the suit.

In ***Devinder Kumar v. Smt. Chatro Devi, AIR 1966 Punj 502*** – It was observed that where the decrease in the light and air in appellant's room was not to such an appreciable extent as would injure the property of appellant in point of value, comfort, convenience or usefulness it cannot be held that appellant has suffered substantial damage by the construction of the walls and roof in front of the window on the second storey.

Q19. When is a right of easement extinguished? Enumerate the circumstances which result in the extinction of easement?

Or

When can the right to the immovable property be extinguished?

Ans: Sections 37 to 47 of the Indian Easements Act deal with the extinction of easements. The circumstances under which easements extinguished are as under:-

1. **From a Cause This Preceded the Imposition of Easement –** Section 37 lays down that when from a cause that preceded

the imposition of an easement, the person it was imposed ceases to have any right in the servient heritage, the easement is extinguished.

The Section lays down a general principle that anybody who has a contingent or limited interest in the servient tenement can grant the easement that would terminate with his own name.

Illustration – 'A' transfers Sultanpur to 'B', on condition that he does not marry 'C' B imposes an easement in Sultanpur. Then 'B' marries 'C'. B's interest in Sultanpur ends and with it, the easement is extinguished.

2. **By Release Express or Implied** – Section 38 says that easement is extinguished when the dominant owner releases it expressly or impliedly,

    Express release:- An easement may be created by an express grant so that easements may be extinguished by express release. An express release can occur by a declaration, oral or written, because no statute requires an express release to be written.

    Implied release: – Just as the grant of the easement may be presumed from the parties' conduct, the release of an easement by the dominant owner may, in certain circumstances, be implied. The release of an easement will be implied:-

    a. Where the dominant owner 'expressly' authorises an act of permanent nature to be done, on the servient heritage, the necessary consequence of which is to 'prevent his future enjoyment of the easement, and such act is done in pursuance of such authority.

b. Where any permanent alteration is made in the dominant heritage of such a nature, as to show that the dominant owner intended to cease to enjoy the easement in future.

3. **By revocation**:- Section 39 lays down that an easement is extinguished when the servient owner in exercise of a power reserved in this behalf, revokes the easement.

4. **On the expiration of the limited period of happening of dissolving condition**:- Where an easement is imposed for a limited period or is acquired on condition that it shall become void on the performance or non-performance of a specified act, then such an easement would extinguish on the expiration of the limited period or on the fulfilment of the contingent condition. This provision is given in Section 40 of the Indian Easement Act.

5. **On termination of necessity**:- Section 41 provides that an easement of necessity is extinguished when the necessity comes to an end. This section codifies the principle that an easement of necessity does not last longer than a necessity. Easements of necessity are those easements that are absolutely necessary for the enjoyment of the dominant heritage. When the absolute necessity ceases and the dominant heritage can be enjoyed without such easement, the easement extinguishes.

6. **On becoming useless**:- Section 42 says that when an easement causes loss of any benefit to the dominant owner under any circumstances and places an unnecessary burden on the servient tenement, then the easement extinguishes.

7. **By permanent change in dominant heritage**:- Section 43 provides that an easement, other than easement of supports is extinguished in the following circumstances which must co-exist:-

i. There must be a permanent change in the dominant heritage;

ii. in consequence of that permanent change the burden on the servient heritage must have been materially increased; and

iii. the increased burden, i.e., the excessive use of the easement, cannot be reduced by the servant owner without interfering with the lawful enjoyment of the easement.

8. **On permanent alteration of servient heritage by superior force**:- Section 44 lays down that where a superior force permanently alters the servient tenement in such a way that the dominant owner can no longer enjoy his easement right, the easement is extinguished. But an exception has been made in case of an easement by way of necessity, in which case the dominant owner has a right to a fresh way of necessity.

9. **By Destruction of Either Heritage**:- Section 45 provides that an easement is extinguished by complete destruction of a tenement, servient or dominant.

10. **By Unity of Ownership**:- Section 46 lays down that an easement is extinguished when the same person becomes entitled to the absolute ownership of the whole of the dominant and servient heritage. The general rule of law is that easements are extinguished by the operation of the law of the ownership of the dominant and servient tenements becoming absolutely united in one and the same person.

11. **By non-enjoyment**:- Section 47 lays down that an easement is extinguished by non-enjoyment for a period of 20 years.

A discontinuous easement is extinguished when for a like period, it has not been enjoyed as such.

Such period shall be reckoned, in the case of a continuous easement, from the day on which its enjoyment was obstructed by the servient owner, or rendered impossible by the dominant owner, and in case of a discontinuous easement, from the day on which it was last enjoyed by any person a dominant owner :

Q20. When is an easement suspended?

Ans: Suspension of easement – An easement is suspended when the dominant owner becomes entitled to possession of the servient heritage for a limited interest therein or when the servient owner becomes entitled to possession of the dominant heritage for a limited interest therein. [Section 49]

The section lays down that unity of possession of the dominant and servient heritage merely suspends an easement. But the unity of estate would extinguish it as provided in section 46.

Where the occupancy tenant had, by purchase, the right to take water from the landlord's well and the landlord had sub-lease from the occupancy tenants, entered into possession it was held that, on the termination of the sub-lease, the easement to take water, which was suspended under section 49, revived.

The dominant owner, who had an easement of way, took possession of the servient tenement as a lessee it was held that the easement was suspended by unity of possession under section 49.

Q21. What do you understand by the revival of an easement and how can it be brought about?

Ans: Section 51 of the Indian Easement Act provides a rule distinct from English Law on the point. In English Law, suspended easement revives, but easement howsoever extinguished can never revive. In India, an extinguished easement can be divided into two categories:-

Section 51 of Indian Easement Act reads as "An easement extinguished u/s 45 revives (a) when the destroyed heritage is before 20 years have expired restored by alluvion (B) when the destroyed heritage is a servient building and before 20 years have expired such building is rebuilt upon the same site and (c) when destroyed heritage is a dominant building and before 20 years have expired such building is rebuilt upon the same site and in such manner as not to expose a greater burden on servient heritage.

An easement extinguished u/s 46 revives when the grantor bequest by which the unity of ownership was produced is set aside by the decree of a competent Court. A necessary easement extinguished under the same section revives when the unity of ownership ceases from any other cause.

A suspended easement revives if the cause of suspension is removed before the right is extinguished u/s 47."

In *AIR 1967 All. 302* it was observed that an easement may be revived after it has been extinguished by the union of dominant and servient tenements in one owner by their subsequent severance, provided the easement is apparent. If there has been unity of possession, merely an easement which has been thereby suspended will revive on severance of the union, but if there has been unity of seisin for estates in fee simple and not unity of possession, merely all easements are absolutely extinguished and will not revive, unless they are re-created.

Q22. Define 'licence' and point out the difference between a 'licence' and an 'easement'?

Ans: Section 52 of the Indian Easements Act defines licence as follows:-

"Where one person grants to another, or to a definite number of other persons, a right to do or continue to do, in or upon the immovable property of the grantor, something which would, in the absence of such right be an interest in the property the right is called the licence."

The term 'easement' has been defined under Section 4 of the Indian Easements Act, as follows:-

"An easement is a right which the owner or occupier of certain land possesses as such, for the beneficial enjoyment of that land, to do and continue to do something, or to prevent and continue to prevent something being done in or upon, in respect of certain other land not his own."

The distinction between easement and licence is given as under -

Licence	Easement
1. Licence is not apparent to any land	1. but is a personal right to do on the grantor's land, which would be unlawful without such licence.
2. A licence is a personal right granted to an individual or ascertained number of individuals.	2. An easement is a right of beneficial enjoyment of property.
3. A licence is not transferable except in the circumstances mentioned in Section 56	3. An Easement right follows the dominant tenement

4. The transferee of the land over which the licence is available is not bound by the Licence	4. The transferee of the servient tenement takes the tenement subject to the easement right
5. A licence is always bound to be of a positive nature	5. An easement right may be positive or negative.
6. A Licence can be revoked at the will of the grantor except in two cases mentioned in Section 60	6. An Easement cannot be revoked at the will of the servient owner.

Q23. What are the main features of a Licence?

Ans: Main features of licence:

1. **It is a privilege of liberty and not right** – Licence is the privilege of the grantee to do something he would have otherwise been not authorised to do. This privilege never matures into a right and continues till the grantor likes it. It can be withdrawn at any time without any notice to the grantee who can never get it enforced in a Court of Law.

2. **It is purely personal** – Licence is personal to the grantee. It touches no property.

3. **It is always positive** – Licence makes lawful the commission or continuation of something being done by the grantee. The licence covers only those wrongs that are limited to the grantor's property and the licence can authorise that. It is never negative.

4. **It is not an interest in property** – Licence is in respect of property but does not amount to an interest in the property in respect of which it is granted. If the property is sold to

somebody, it goes free from all the liabilities accepted or imposed by licence.

5. **Non-transferable and non-heritable** – Licensee can not transfer the licence or goes down to heirs after the licensee's death.

The definite number of persons to hold licence – The High Court of J. and K. has held in the case of ***ShambhoNath v. Kapoor Singh, A.I.R. 1976 J. and K. 52*** that under section 52 of the Easements Act, the licence can be granted only in favour of the definite number of persons and not in favour of fluctuating body of individuals. Even if binding on the defendants, the agreement involved in the case cannot be considered to be at best a bilateral agreement between the representatives of the two parties and containing reciprocal conditions.

In ***E.P. George v. Thomas John AIR 1984 Ker. 224*** it was observed, "A licence properly passes no interest nor alters or transfers the property in anything but only makes action lawful without which it would be unlawful. From the definition of Section 52, it is clear that the licensee has no interest in the property and his possession for the enjoyment of his right is not judicial possession but only occupation.

Q23. Distinguish between lease and licence.

Ans: The distinction between lease and licence Section 105 of the Transfer of Property Act defines lease. A lease of immovable property is the transfer of a right to enjoy such property, made for a certain time express or implied, or in perpetuity, in consideration of a price paid or promised, or of money, a share of crops, services or any other thing of value to be rendered, periodically or on specified occasions to the transferor by the transferee, who accepts the transfer on such terms.

1. The main point of distinction between a lease and licence is regarding the exclusive possession of the property if the effect of the agreement is to give exclusive possession to the holder; though subject to certain reservations, then it is a lease; if the agreement is merely for the use property in a certain way and on certain terms, while it remains, in possession of the owner, it is a licence. (***Sharif Dadumiya v. Emperior, 32 Bom. L.R. 332***).

2. The cardinal distinction between a lease and a licence is that there is a transfer of an interest in land in a lease, whereas, in the case of a licence, there is no transfer of interest, although the licensee acquires a right to occupy the land. For example, where A agreed with B to let him use the Surety Garden and Music Hall for four days at Rs. 100 per day to give a series of concerts etc., it was held that it was not letting and there was no tenancy as there was no transfer of an interest in the land although the contract gave the licensee the use of the hall and garden for a specified time.

3. A lease can be assigned to a third person while a licence cannot be assigned.

4. A lease can bring an action for trespass, and he can also maintain a suit for possession when a licensee cannot.

5. A lease is not revocable, a licence is revocable.

6. A lessee forfeits the lease and becomes liable to ejectment if he denies the grantor's title while a licensee does not.

7. A lease needs registration. A grant of licence needs no registration.

Q24. Who may grant a licence?

Ans: According to Section 53 of the Act -

"A licence may be granted by anyone in the circumstances and to the extent in and to which he may transfer his interest in property affected by the licence."

So section 53 lays down with regard to the power to grant a licence. Circumstances in which and the extent to which a licence may be granted are the circumstances in which and the extent to which the grantor of the licence may transfer his interest in the property.

Thus whereas a co-owner would not be entitled without the consent of other co-owners to grant an easement, he would be entitled to grant a licence in respect of the property in which he may have a right as a co-owner as far as the grant of such licence would not amount to an unreasonable user of the joint property.

Where G and A were co-owner of a forest and G mortgaged his interest with possession to the plaintiff and then both G and A licensed a third person to cut and take wood from the forest on a suit by the plaintiff mortgagee, it was held that A being the co-owner, had a right to grant the licence but not G who was out of possession [***Balvantrav v. Ganpatrav, ILR 7 Bom. 336***].

Q25. When is a licence deemed to be revoked?

Ans: A licence is deemed to be revoked as per Section 62:-

a. Where from a cause preceding the grant of it, the grantor ceases to have any interest in the property covered by the licence.

b. When the licensee releases it, expressly or impliedly, to the grantor or his representative.

c. When it has been granted for a limited period or acquired on condition that it shall become void on the performance or non-performance of a specified act and, the period expires, or the condition is fulfilled.

d. Where the property affected by the licence is destroyed or by superior force permanently altered that the licensee can no longer exercise his right.

e. When the licensee becomes entitled to the absolute ownership of the property affected by his right.

f. When the licence is granted for a specified purpose and the purpose is attained, or abandoned or becomes impracticable.

g. Where the licence is granted to the licensee as holding a particular office, employment or character, and such office, employment or character ceases to exist.

h. Where the licence ceases to be used as such for an unbroken period of twenty years, and such cessation is not in pursuance of a contract between the grantor and the licensee.

i. In the case of an accessory licence, when the interest or right to which it is necessary ceases to exist.

Section 62 is another section laying down the very important principle of law. It deals with nine specified situations in which the revocation of the licence shall be presumed. The section provides that the existence of any of the nine circumstances will come by itself be sufficient to allow to presume that the relevant licence has been properly revoked. Nothing else is necessary.

In AIR 1953 All. 439, it was observed that Section 60 deals with a case when the licence is revoked at the will of the Licensor. Section 62 enumerates the circumstances on the happening of any one of which a licence is revoked. Each clause of Section 62 is independent of the other and by itself constitutes the ground for deeming a licence to have revoked.

CHAPTER 17

DEVELOPMENT CONTROL AND PROMOTIONS REGULATION 2034

Bombay, also known as the supreme city which has thousands of people pouring in every day. While the number of residents increases tremendously, the city has limited geography to deal with. That is where land laws and Development Control Regulations (DCR) play a significant role. Development Control and Promotion Regulation (DCPR) is a public document that has the rules and regulations for all kinds of ongoing and future real estate developments in the city. Owing to its significance, DCPR is a comprehensive document expressed with a rigorous and complete analysis of the city's infrastructure, demographics, financial and economic environment. With the release of DCPR 2034, the former level of uncertainty has ended. The developer community can now develop with confidence. The policy delivers clarity and focuses on the future development of the Mumbai state. The DCPR 2034 has given an enhancement to the commercial sector in Mumbai by way of incentivized FSI, yet, the high cost of the FSI could be an issue. On the residential front, events such as opening up of land for endorsing affordable housing and unification of carpet area will prove to be an advantage for home-buyers

Q1. What are the vital activities of the Building Permission Department?

Ans: The key activities of the department are:

a. To permit new building construction

b. To extend sanction for the erection of the new building

c. To extend sanction to for extension/ remodelling/renovation of existing building

d. Delivery of certified copy of plans.

e. To stop unauthorized construction

f. To demolish unauthorized construction

g. To keep vigilance against any heritage building

h. To take rational action against insecure buildings.

Q2. What is the way to attain building permission on land that is within the MCGM limit?

Ans: For obtaining Building permission, we need to apply online with all documents and proposed project predict drawing.

- Need to assign architect to get building permission from MCGM architect.

- After assigning architect need to apply online through his login console, where he fills in all required details to get Building permission

- After attaching an essential document and drawing with scrutiny, fees file/Application will be submitted to MCGM

- Submitted File/Application inward in define authority where actual site allocated

- Concern officer scrutinized proposal documents, proposed drawing, and Actual site visit

- And get approval on the same from higher authority.

Q3. What is the duration of the validity period for Building Permission?

Ans: Building Permission approved by MCGM is valid for a year. However, it can be renewed for another year; subsequently, a new permission is needed if the building is not constructed by this time.

Q4. What is the Penalty that can be imposed if a building is constructed without approval or there is a violation of the approved plan?

Ans: Penalty set by MCGM is Building Permission fees can be levied in these cases as per rules and regulation.

Q5. Along with the application which documents are necessary?

Ans: Documents required are varied case to case depending upon the type of permission (Layout, addition/deletion/alteration of existing building), proposed Building usage (residential, commercial, mix, or industrial)

- Notice u/s 302/337/342 of MMC Act.
- Notice u/s 44/69 MRTP act 1966
- Owners Affidavit
- Ownership title document – conveyance deed
- Property Register card (Area in words)
- Sale/ lease deed/ power of attorney
- Structural stability report (if existing structure retained)
- Tax clearance certificate Additions, Alterations
- The documents showing the authenticity of the structures proposed to be retained were an extension to the structure,

either vertical or horizontal, is proposed to ascertain that the structure which is proposed to be reserved is not unauthorized.

- Title clearance certificate from Solicitor and PAN card
- E. Survey Remarks
- B-form (if plot under T.P. scheme)
- Copy of approved layout/subdivision/amalgamation along with term & conditions
- Copy of change of user permission from I to R/C1 issued by DP section wherever applicable
- Copy of development permission issued by DP Section if the land is under reservation
- Architect Area Certificate By triangulation
- Copy of right of way
- Index
- Kami Jasti Patra (KJP)
- Copy of TP remarks (in case of the plot is in TP scheme)
- P. Remark
- Development agreement
- Development Plan
- DILR sketch measurement plan /city survey sheet
- Exemption order/clearance order/sale permission/ redevelopment permission ULC
- Gut book sketch
- In case a plot is to be developed by deriving a "right of way", a registered agreement from the concerned owner

- In the case of Government / M.C.G.M. land, NOC from collector or Concerned authority of the Government / Estate dept of M.C.G.M
- Indemnity bond (for ULC)

Q6. Along with the application, what is the fees to be paid, and at what rate will it be paid after approval?

Ans: Along with the application Scrutiny fees is to be paid and all fees as per particulars shown in "MCGM [DCR]"

Q7. After the application duly made in what time frame we can start construction on-site?

Ans: After approval of the Building Permission application. (for which the maximum specified period is distinct in which decision regarding approval is granted)

Q8. Before making any application for Building Permission which other Departments' consultation or NOC is mandatory?

Ans:

a. A. For internal MCGM departmental NOC's provision is made in the online system to get departmental NOC by applying online at the time building permission request application.

b. B. Apart from MCGM departments remark some external government bodies are also linked to get online remarks/ NOC through online building permission request application

- District-collector office for non-agriculture (NA) order/ approval.
- Approval from the Airport Authority of India (NOC is required for height clearance of buildings/structures/

masts from the directorate of air traffic management, Airport Authority of India (AAI), when the project lies within 20 km. The radius of airstrips/ funnel.

- NOC from coastal zone management authority. (NOC is required when the land is near the coast as construction is not allowed up to 500 meters from the high tide line.)

- Approval from the national monument authority (NOC required from the National Monument Authority (NMA) / Archaeological Survey of India (ASI) when the entire project site

- Or part/s of it is within a 300-meter radius from the declared boundary of any monument protected under the ancient monument act and is under the control of ASI.

- Approval from the Maharashtra heritage conservation committee (NOC required from the Maharashtra heritage conservation committee (MHCC) or appropriate authority when the project has any link/ relation with any listed heritage building or within their compound limit.

- Approval from railway authority/port trust/defence (NOC is required from the railway authority/Mumbai port trust/defence when the project site is along the railway corridor / within the jurisdiction of Mumbai port trust, respectively.

- Approval from road owning agency (PWD for national highway/state highway/another major-minor road regarding building-control-line opinion)

- Approval from the chief controller of explosives (approval is required from the chief controller of explosives, Nagpur in case of hazardous building or storing hazardous materials in the building(s).)

- Approval is required from the chief inspector of factories in the case of an industrial building.

- Environment clearance is required from the ministry of environment and forests (MEF)/ state-level expert committee for all building/construction projects having built-up area more than 20000 square meters and area development projects/townships covering an area of more than 50 hectares or built-up area more than 1, 50,000 square meters.

- Approval from the local body (approval is required from the local body/authority (MCGM/MMRDA/NMCC) to sanction building plans/ building permit under the provisions of building bylaws, master plan, and local body acts. The local body forwards the proposals to the various other concerned authorities in the city as required for case-specific approvals/ NOC before granting a building permit.

- Approval from DCP (licensing)(police Dept. (for cinema /theatre/multiplex /hotel/ religious building/ fuelling stations/party plot etc.)

- Approval is required from the power distributing / supply agency (BEST/Tata/MSEDCL)

- Oil and gas pipeline depth. (if under passing or have rights in the land of building unit)

Q9. How to obtain a certified approved opinion/plan of building unit from authority?

Ans: The Zoning certificate, D.P. part-plan, and T.P. Scheme Part Plan, From-F (viewing area, ownership & additional details as per T.P. scheme) from Authority [MCGM] office by paying due fees.

Q10. What is the procedure to obtain approval of Building in Authority?

Ans:

- Accomplish online application in the due procedure as mentioned on MCGM.gov.in.
- After intimation of any compliance demand regarding application online from an authority, please make necessary compliance along with the online proposal.
- Thus, the application procedure is completed.
- Within the due frame of time of 90 days, the decision regarding the application is issued /intimated. Thus, the application is principally approved, subjected to due fees payments and the issue of the Approval Certificate.

Q11. How do Building Permit processes works in MCGM?

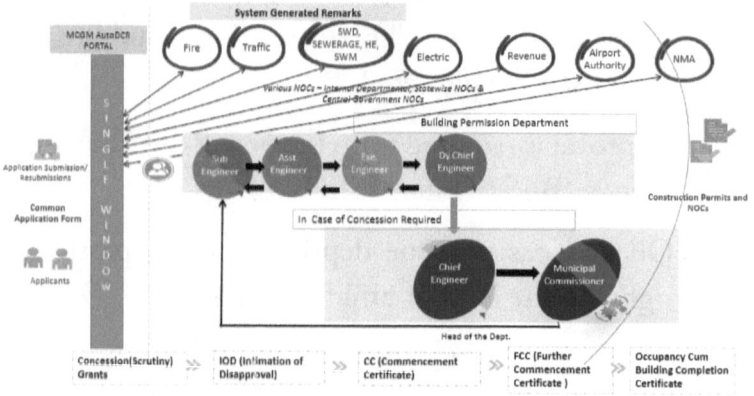

Q12. What is FSI?

Ans: Floor Space Index (FSI) is the proportion of the developed space on a plot to the zone of the plot. It is a guideline followed in the development control standards of numerous urban communities to control their densification and development design. In numerous Indian urban communities, the FSI dispersion is free of land accessibility and densities. All in all, FSI estimations of Indian urban areas are low when contrasted with different urban communities on the planet, in this way keeping the per capita manufactured space low.

Q13. Does FSI vary from city to city?

Ans: FSI is a typical variable in urban areas and results in shifting examples of urban structure and space development. It is also a device for organizers to control the degree of the developed zone on a given plot and a valuation instrument in real estate advertising. In some huge urban areas like Delhi, Bengaluru, and Kolkata, it is known as Floor Area Region (FAR), and in certain urban areas like Mumbai and Chennai, it is known as Floor Space Index (FSI).

These elements increment the FSI from regularly admissible FSI.

For instance, in the National Capital Region (NCR), the passable FSI is somewhere in the range of 1.2 and 3.5, according to the Delhi Master Plan strategy 2021. Be that as it may, it energizes higher FSI and tallness along 500m on the two sides from the inside line of MRTS/significant vehicle hall reserved as an impacted zone. Redevelopment ventures are likewise conceded a most extreme FSI estimation of 4. For private plots in NCR, the FSI diminishes as the plot size increments.

Bengaluru has likewise embraced TOD guidelines for plots adjoining 60m or more street width and inside 150m sweep of any travel centre point, giving an extra FSI of 0.5 far beyond typically passable FSI. There is no distinction in FSI variety in private and business plots. The most extreme FSI incorporating the extra FSI in the TOD zone can be accomplished greatest up to four.

In Mumbai, for residential growth, the FSI is uniform over the entire zone, independent of plot size and building movement. The FSI shifts from 0.5 in the suburban area to 1.33 in the Island city. It additionally offers higher FSI up to 2.5 and 2.5 in addition to impetuses for the development and redevelopment of MAHADA individually. With the relevance of TDR and premium FSI, the FSI can be proficient up to 5.

Hyderabad has not put FSI limitations. In particular, tall structures have a free-FSI (no restriction on FSI) to empower developments in the city. Be that as it may, according to the Andhra Pradesh building rules, the developed region sometimes, for example, ventured type, platform, and tower structures were being done platform, FSI of up to 5. The MA and UD office is anyway bearing in mind the reintroduction of floor space index (FSI) standard for elevated structures in the state of Telangana.

Q14. How would the FSI increase the impact on the industry?

Ans: The expansion does not represent any effect for littler plots underneath 700 sq.m, subject to the relevance of difficulties, tallness limitations as far as the number of floors. Since it is suitable just in the private division, land developers and proprietors will be hasty to adapt land with private developments. Further, greater clearness is required for unique structures falling under classifications B and C individually.

The new principles will clear a path for new and redevelopment ventures, promising vertical development. Additional FSI will affect land esteems or possibly selling costs of created resources. Developers or the land proprietors who have just gone into development understandings or developers who have bought land for development will be quick inheritors. Littler land packages are probably going to have an extremely insignificant effect dissimilar to bigger ones. Since the FSI increment is centred around the private segment, developers will probably focus more on the development of private undertakings than business resources and concentrate benefits. We could see the opening of numerous potential land packages, both in downtown areas and rural areas. The present infra-and flow-physical framework, for example, water flexibly, sewerage, conveying limit of the streets, and so on., including stopping, would require more growth as they could be stressed mostly in downtown areas.

Typically, the built-up area is the space covered by all the floors in a building and is primarily dependent on the Floor Space Index (FSI). For example, if the total land area is 2,000 sq ft and the FSI set by the government is 3, then the builder can construct up to 6,000 sq ft of floor space on the accessible plot.

Q15. What is the formula for calculating built-up area?

Ans: Built-up Area= Plot Area x FSI

Built-up Area = 2,000 sq ft x 3= 6,000 sq ft

Q16. What is fungible FSI?

Ans: However, if the developer wants to construct anything beyond the permissible FSI limit and increase the built-up area beyond 6,000 sq ft, they have to purchase the space from the city authorities. The extra space bought from the authorities is referred to as fungible FSI. It is also referred to as Premium FSI.

As per the rule, the fungible FSI should not surpass more than 35 percent of the floor area in residential properties and 20 percent of the floor area in industrial and commercial developments. Everything beyond the purchased space is considered unlawful, and the builder can face severe consequences such as heavy fines.

Q17. What is the amended fungible FSI as per the new DCR?

Ans: The concept of 'Fungible FSI' was amended in the new Development Control Regulations (DPCR) in 2012, wherein the areas such as balconies, flower beds, terraces, and niches were included under the FSI. To compensate the builders for the loss, the government made a provision of additional built-up space instead of a premium.

The premium imposed is a proportion of the Ready Reckoner Rate (RRR) predominant in that area. For instance, residential properties attract 60 percent of the RRR as a fungible FSI fee. Likewise, the fees imposed for industrial and commercial developments are 80 and 100 percent of RRR, respectively.

Also, to avail of the fungible FSI, the road adjoining the plot must be at least 30 ft wide. Below is the breakdown of the fungible FSI according to the neighbouring road width.

Road width	Permissible Fungible FSI in Residential Properties
30-40 ft	20 percent
40-60 ft	30 percent
More than 60 ft	35 percent

For instance

If the land area is 2,000 sq. ft and the FSI is 2, and the adjoining road width is 35 ft, then the builder can avail 20 percent additional floor space as fungible FSI.

Additional built-up area here would be:

Built-up Area x Fungible FSI

(2,000 sq. ft x 2) x 20/100 = 800 sq. ft

Floor space allowed in total = 4,000+800 = 4,800 sq. ft

Now, the builder can construct up to 4,800 sq. ft of floor space.

The FSI and the fungible FSI in an area vary as per the type of building one plan to construct. To understand the prevalent FSI and the fungible FSI in the favoured area, one needs to visit the State government's official website to assist in better planning and execution.

Q18. What is meant by the concept TDR?

Ans:

- Transfer of Development Rights (TDR) implies making an accessible, certain measure of extra-developed territory instead of the zone surrendered or gave up by the proprietor of the land, with the goal that he can utilize the extra-developed zone either himself or transfer it to another needing the extra-developed region for a concurred aggregate of cash.

- Transferable Development Rights or TDR can be considered a significant raw material in the real estate business. It permits the developer to work far beyond the reasonable Floor Space Index (FSI) under the pervasive guidelines of the particular areas. On the back of developing urbanization and the absence of accessibility of space, TDR expects a more noteworthy significance, particularly in the rural regions of the urban areas.

- When the Legislature attempts to secure individual land packages for making infrastructural ventures, it is required to repay the land proprietors. The compensation given by the Administration is typically lower than the market rate, and thus they presented the idea of Transferable Development

Rights. These rights are gotten as authentications, which the proprietor can use for himself or can exchange the market for the money.

- Based on the development phase, a city is characterized into different zones like completely grew, tolerably created, and inadequately created. The Transferable Development Rights are normally transferred from the completely evolved zones to different zones and not the other way around. For instance, on account of a city like Mumbai, the TDR which is produced in the island city (for example southern part), will be used for development in the suburban territories (for example northern part). The fundamental standard of such usage is likewise to encourage the development of the underdeveloped regions.

Q19. What are the types of TDR?

Ans: Primarily, four types of TDR are granted –

- Road TDR
- Slum TDR
- Heritage TDR
- Reserved plots TDR

Q20. What is TDR MARKET?

Ans: Like the stock markets, urban areas like Mumbai have a colossal TDR advertise set up. As these TDR certificates can be exchanged in the market for money, most developers buy the equivalent and expand their admissible development rights. TDR exchanging follows the open market guideline wherein the valuing is determined by request, gracefully and accessibility and there is no Administration power over the equivalent. In the greater part of the cases, a normal individual does not become more acquainted with the way TDR is purchased, sold, or executed.

Q21. What is the 7/12 extract Document?

Ans: The 7/12 extract is an information document prescribing details about a specific piece of land such as survey number, area, date, and more particulars about the existing owner›s name. This extract is a combination of 2 forms. Form 7 talks about the details of the landowners and their rights while Form 12 lists specifics about the land type and usage. ‹Saat-Baara-Utara' is the regional term for the 7/12 Extract Document in Maharashtra. The revenue department of the state maintains the document for tax collection purposes. The concerned land authority or tehsildar usually issues the extract. Buyer can get a copy of the document after paying the official fee or file a petition under the Right to Information Act to get the copy.

Q22. Why is 7/12 Extract important?

Ans: 7/12 extract Documents is a significant indicator of the legal status of the plot. It is used for finding relevant details about the ancestral information of any specific land. Former disputes, court orders, litigation etc. that could affect the land ownership or its lawful stature can be found in this document. Apart from this, 7/12 extract is a record of all the activities done on the land earlier. It is important to document identifying the land to establish the exact location and its physical nature. For agricultural land, the extract also keeps a record of the last grown crops on the land.

Q23. Describe Land Use Zoning under DCPR?

Ans: Wherein there is the development of any land, the permissible uses of the land zone should be confirmed.

Q24. What are the different Zones mentioned under the Act?

Ans: Broadly as mentioned under the DCPR there are 3 types of Zones. They are as follows-

- Residential Zones
- Commercial Zones
- Industrial Zones
- Special Development Zone
- Port Operational Zone
- Natural Zones
- Green Zone

Q25. Describe Residential Zone under DCPR?

Ans: Residential Zone under DCPR is represented by "R". The Residential Zone is a mixed-use zone with residential use as the major one and where other uses as specified are permitted.

Q26. Describe Special Development Zone under DCPR?

Ans: Special Development Zone under DCPR is represented by "SDZ". Special Development Zone (SDZ) is a zone that is to be developed predominantly for society, emphasising Affordable Housing, POS, and necessary Social infrastructures.

Q27. Describe Natural Zones under DCPR?

Ans: Natural Zone under DCPR is represented by "NA". Natural Area Zone (NA) is an environmentally sensitive zone amenable to buildable development with the approval of the Competent Authority.

Q28. List the various conditions under which Land-use and Occupancies are permissible?

Ans: The various conditions under which Land-use and Occupancies are permissible are as follows-

1. Independent plot
2. Independent building
3. Separate wing with separate access
4. Separate floor with separate access
5. On the ground floor
6. On the ground floor with separate access.
7. On stilt
8. On the top of the podium
9. On-ground/stilt, 1st & 2nd floors with separate access
10. On Terrace
11. Minimum area of plot-1,000 sq. m
12. Minimum area of plot-2,500 sq. m
13. Minimum width of the street on which the plot abuts-9.00 m
14. Minimum width of the street on which the plot abuts-12.00m
15. Minimum width of the street on which the plot abuts-13.40m
16. Minimum width of the street on which the plot abuts-18.30m
17. Permissible on the street on which the plot abuts road having width more than 18.3 m excepting roads as stated in regulation below this table
18. All ancillary uses limited to 50% floor space of principal use

19. Minimum width of side & rear marginal open Space-6.0m.

20. 20. In a single-storeyed detached or semi-detached structure each unit having an area of not more than 100 sq. m

21. With the Special permission of Commissioner

22. Subject to permission of Commissioner of Police

23. Subject to approval from Traffic Police.

24. Subject to permission from Executive Health Officer of MGM.

25. Subject to permission from Director of Industries

26. Subject to permission from Controller of Explosives.

27. Minimum width of side & rear marginal Open Space – 9.0m.

28. By maintaining segregating distances as per Regulation No 41

Q29. Discuss Special Development Zones?

Ans: Special Development Zones are such zones that are developed to benefit society at large and focus more on affordable housing for all, the necessary infrastructure for social development. Special Development Zones are guided under Regulation 33(8).

Q30. Discuss other development in Special Development Zones?

Ans: Some of the other developments in Special Development Zones are as follows-

- Institutional Development Centre
- Development on Cinemas and TV film production
- Information Technology
- Tourism Development Area

Q31. Describe Natural Areas under DCPR?

Ans: Natural Areas are environmentally sensitive zones that can be used for development after taking necessary approvals from the appropriate Authority.

Q32. What sort of developmental activities are permissible for development?

Ans: The following facilities are permissible-

- Boardwalks in mangroves, trekking facilities, Public Sanitary, Conveniences for visitors, Sewerage Pumping Station.
- Uses permissible as per the notifications issued by the Ministry of Environment and Forest, if any, as amended from time to time.

Q33. Discuss Green Zones under DCPR?

Ans: Green zones under DCPR are a large piece of lands which are predominantly of green cover.

Q34. What sort of developmental activities are permissible for development under Green Zone?

Ans: The developmental activities that are permissible for developments under Green Zone are as follows-

- Construction of Zoo with FSI of 0.025
- Uses approved by the appropriate government with permission from the Ministry of Environment and Forest
- Rehabilitation & Resettlement of the original residents of the forest.

Q35. Describe the Fire protection Requirements under DCPR?

Ans: Fire protection Requirements are necessary to ensure that the building has taken customers' safety and ensures safety from fire.

Q36. Discuss the provisions related to fire protection in high-rise buildings?

Ans: The provisions related to fire protection in the high-rise buildings are as follows-

- If the buildings have a height of more than 32 m up to 70 m, at least one side other than the roadside shall have clear open space.
- If the buildings have a height of more than 70 m, at least one side other than the roadside shall have clear open space.

Q37. Discuss the construction materials to be used?

Ans: The materials used for constructing a building should be fire-resistant as it will ensure safety for the customers.

Q38. Discuss Exits under the Urban Safety Requirements under DCPR?

Ans: Exits under the Urban Safety Requirements means that every building which is constructed for human occupancy must have sufficient to permit the safe escape of its occupants in case of fire.

Q39. Discuss Structural Design under the Urban Safety Requirements under DCPR?

Ans: Structural Design under the Urban Safety Requirements is important because the building stands on such designs. The structural design should comply with Indian Standard Codes of structural design for structural safety.

Q40. Describe the various structural design standards for Structural Safety?

Ans: The various structural designs standards for Structural Safety are as follows-

- Indian Standard Code of Practice for Earthquake Resistant Design IS1893
- Indian Standard Seismic Code of Practice for Seismic Design IS1893
- Indian Standard Code of Practice for Wind Pressure
- IS Code as would be made applicable by Bureau of Indian Standard from time to time

Q41. Describe Conservation, Preservation & Restoration of Heritage Properties under DCPR?

Ans: Conservation refers to the processes of looking after a place to retain its history and includes maintenance, preservation, restoration, reconstruction, and adoption or a combination of more than one of these.

Preservation means and comprises of sustaining the fabric of a place in its prevailing state and retarding deterioration.

Restoration means returning the existing fabric of a place to a known earlier state by removing deposits or reassembling existing components.

Q42. Discuss the Restrictions on Development/Re-development/Repairs of Heritage Properties?

Ans: The Restrictions on Development/Re-development/Repairs of Heritage Properties are as follows-

1. Regarding heritage buildings, development/alterations/repairs/ restoration shall be by the provisions mentioned at 9 (C & D) of this regulation.

2. In exceptional cases, for reasons to be recorded in writing, using his powers of special permission, the Commissioner of the Municipal corporation's decision on the same shall be final.

3. Concerning religious buildings, the changes, repairs, additions, alterations, and renovations required on religious grounds mentioned in sacred texts shall be treated as permissible, subject to their being in accordance and consonance with the original structure and architecture designs, aesthetics, and other special features thereof.

Q43. Describe the Development plan reservation?

Ans: If any sort of Development plan Reservations on listed heritage structure and due to development of such site if adversely affects its character, then Municipal Commissioner shall initiate the process of modification of such reservation following due procedure.

Q44. Describe the Coastal Regulation Zone under DCPR?

Ans: The development within CRZ areas shall be governed by the Coastal Regulation Zone Notifications provided by the Ministry of Environment and Forest, Government of India. Lands showed as Natural Area in Development Plans and situated on the seaward side of High Tide Line, if the modification to High Tide Line, falls on the landward side of altered High Tide Line, then in such instance, the said land will be considered to have been located in the zone of adjoining land.

Q45. Describe the Restrictions on Development in certain areas?

Ans: The following are the Restrictions on Development in certain areas:

- Funnel of Vision
- Height restrictions in the vicinity of aerodromes
- Building sites abutting railway track boundary
- Distance from electricity lines
- Other restrictions in height
- Restriction on Development of sites of existing Fuel Stations
- Structures not included in reckoning height

Q46. What are the key DCPR 2034 provisions impacting the residential segment?

Ans: They are as follows

1. The DCPR 2034 simplifies the construction of taller buildings by connecting the permissible floor space index (FSI) to the road width. Former policies have been limited to inspect congestion, leading to the construction of tall residential or commercial towers, on narrower roads.

2. Increase in the FSI through the increase in Transfer of Development Rights (TDR) limits. This increase in FSI stems from an increase in FSI upon payment of premium and the increase in the significance of TDR that can be encumbered on the plot, thus increasing revenue generation for the municipal corporations and the government.

3. The DCPR 2034 has increased development rights for areas surrendered to the BMC. This was increased to 2.5 times the area of land surrendered in the city and 2 times the area of land

surrendered in the outskirts, thereby motivating stakeholders to quicken the development of slum rehabilitation and surrendering of reserved plots.

4. The reduction of consent requirements for the redevelopment of ceased and MHADA buildings from 70 percent to 51 percent. While this reduction may not completely address the issue of redevelopment projects caught in the litigation, it helps begin the projects having a majority consent of home owners.

Q47. What are the key DCPR 2034 provisions impacting the commercial segment?

Ans: They are as follows

1. If the road width is more than 12 meters, then the DCPR 2034 offers higher FSI for office developments. The idea behind this is to decrease traffic congestion around commercial complexes since the frequency and number of vehicles moving in and out of the commercial building throughout the day is higher than residential spaces.

2. The DCPR 2034 aims to create eight million jobs in Mumbai by increasing the supply of office spaces. The additional FSI aims to encourage commercial development, over residential development, which can be purchased from the BMC, by paying a premium at the rate of 50 percent of the Annual Schedule of Rates ASR. The current set of incentives in the form of additional FSI, may not adequately promote office developments, to the extent required.

CHAPTER 18

SLUM REHABILITATION AUTHORITY

India is on an accelerated path of urbanization and several Indian cities face the challenge of housing their growing population, especially the urban poor. Most of the population is forced to live in slums, especially in large cities like Mumbai.

As per a study conducted in 2011, 62% of Mumbai's population lives in slums. Asia's largest slum, Dharavi is situated in Mumbai. Numerous massive slums are also found in the outskirts. To overcome this, the State of Maharashtra passed The Maharashtra Slum Areas (Improvement Clearance and Redevelopment) Act, 1971 also called "**the Slum Act**".

Under the Slum Act, the Slum Rehabilitation Authority (**SRA**) was formed and comprises of a Chairperson (Chief Minister of Maharashtra) and a Chief Executive Officer of the Authority is a super time scale IAS Officer along with other members being Ministers, elected members of the State Legislature, Secretaries of the concerned State Government and some non-official members who are professionals in the field of construction, planning, architecture, social services, etc. and tasked to finish all the requirements under the Act including survey and review slums, frame the scheme under section 3-B of the Slum Act known as 'Slum Rehabilitation Scheme(**SRS**) for rehabilitation and redevelopment of slums, execution of such schemes, stating any area as slum and fit for rehabilitation, etc.

Before implementing an SRS, the SRA has to declare an area as a Slum Area which means any area which may be a source of danger to the health, safety, or accessibility of the public of that area, or has no basic facilities, or is overcrowded, or unfit for human habitation or harmful to the health, safety or convenience of the public. Once this step is accomplished, an SRS can be started.

Q1. What will be the benefit of this Act for the Developer and the dweller?

Ans: Once the slum dwellers and the SRA have appointed the Developer, all the eligible slum dwellers get free of cost self-contained unit for their residence, which is called the Rehab Component. As this legislation is meant to benefit slum dwellers, they are not allowed to transfer or sell their flat or create any third-party rights thereupon for at least 10 years.

As the Developer puts in resources in the form of money, men, and material for the construction of free houses for the slum dwellers, the Developer is rewarded for his hard work in the form of the Free Sale Component, which can be commercially utilized. After removing the Rehab Component, the Free Sale component is the entire development potential sanctioned by the authority under the Letter of Intent (LOI).

Q2. How is DCPR and SRA Act beneficial in developing the Slum Areas?

Ans: Regulation 33(10) of the Development Control and Promotion Regulation for Greater Mumbai, 2034 governs the development of the SRS and it is summarized under:

- Formation of housing society by 51% or more slum dwellers and appointment of a suitable developer, who would demarcate the slum area and execute individual agreements with the slum dwellers.

- A proposal enclosing requisite plans, annexures, documents (consents, etc.) is then submitted by the architect, appointed by the Developer, to SRA.

- Initial scrutiny of the proposal by the sub-engineer along with payment of scrutiny fees. Annexures I, II, and III are forwarded to the competent authority for scrutiny and certification.

- After the Certification of Annexure-II and III, the Letter of Intent (LOI) with layout plan is issued by the SRA in favour of the Developer and society, setting out details of the development potential available for rehabilitation and free sale and the conditions relating to development.

- The Developer provides slum dwellers with either rent money or transit accommodation, as per their option, and then their hutments are demolished.

- Intimation of Approval (IOA) and Commencement Certificate (CC) is given to the first building for work up to the plinth level. Construction is done up to the base level and after checking the base dimensions, further permission to carry out construction beyond the base is granted.

- Then the Developer would construct the Rehab Component after which the allotment would take place as per eligibility. If any units persist, the same would be handed over to the Government for free.

- The commencement certificates of the rehab and free sale buildings are granted in proportion to each other. Upon completion of the Rehab Component, a list of allotments is prepared.

- Occupancy Certificate (OC) is granted to the Rehab and the Free Sale buildings and rehab tenements are allotted as per the approved list and identity cards are issued by the SRA.

- Lease of rehab and free sale lands (as stated hereunder) is granted in favour of the society of slum dwellers and the society of flat purchasers/developers, respectively. Separate revenue records are formed for the rehab land and the free sale land. SRA acts as facilitating agency if any challenges arise with the revenue authorities.

Q3. What is the procedure for vesting land?

Ans: As per Section 15A of the Slum Act, within 30 days of completion of the Rehab Component, the CEO shall declare, by notification in the Official Gazette, that the land vests in the SRA, whether the land belongs to the State Government, Municipal Council, BMC or the MHADA, on condition that the SRA obtains a no-objection certificate from such land-owning authority. Such land-owning authority shall be allowed to receive compensation from the SRA for such vesting of land. Subsequently, the SRA shall lease the Rehab Land and the Free Sale Land in favour of slum dwellers and the society of flat purchasers, correspondingly, for 30 years, renewable for a further period of 30 years.

Q4. Discuss Regulation 33(10) concerning Slum Rehabilitation?

Ans: The main objective of Regulation 33(10) concerning Slum Rehabilitation is to provide the person who is eligible to be a slum dweller a free house or shop. The person who develops such rehabilitation things gets a free sale component to subsidize the costs incurred.

Q5. Can a land be used as collateral for such social causes?

Ans: Yes, land can be used as collateral for such social causes under Regulation 33(9).

Q6. What are the facilities that a slum dweller gets under Slum Rehabilitation Schemes?

Ans: the facilities that a slum dweller gets under Slum Rehabilitation Schemes are as follows-

1. A Residential Hut of the area has a 300 sq. ft carpet area for free.
2. A shop in the area has a 225 sq. ft Carpet Area. In case the shop exceeds the free area as provided, the additional area can be purchased at a mutually decided rate.
3. 4 Amenities of 300 sq. ft area for 250 slum tenements.
4. A society office for every 100 Slum Dwellers.
5. A community hall of 2% of rehab BUA, subject to a max of 200 sq. ft.

Q7. What are the restrictions on Slum Dwellers?

Ans: The restrictions on Slum Dwellers under Slum Rehabilitation Schemes are as follows-

1. The Slum Dweller/Tenement cannot sell such properties for 10 years from the date of Allotment.
2. The Property's Ownership is in the Joint name of the Slum Dweller and his Spouse.
3. The Managing Committee Shall also have women members.
4. And the most important thing is that only one Rehab tenement per family.

Q8. Who are all Eligible to be Slum Dwellers under Slum Rehabilitation Schemes?

Ans: The people who are eligible to be Slum Dwellers under Slum Rehabilitation Schemes are as follows:

- A person declared under the Act as a Slum Dweller.
- As of date, anyone staying in a hut existing on 01/01/2000 is eligible for a free house.
- Anyone staying in a hut existing on 01/01/2011 is eligible for the house at a cost as decided by the Government.

Q9. In which Area can a Slum Rehabilitation Scheme be implemented?

Ans: A Slum Rehabilitation Scheme be implemented in areas as follows-

- A plot that is declared as slum rehabilitation area by SRA under section 3(c) of Slum Act.
- The area used for the construction of temporary or permanent transit camps is also a slum rehabilitation area.

Q10. How can a Slum Rehabilitation Scheme be implemented?

Ans: A Slum Rehabilitation Scheme be implemented through following manners:

- It is implemented on Govt. lands with the consent of 51% of Members.
- A premium of 25% of the ASR for the land to be paid.
- NOC to be given by the landowning authority within 60 days of the grant of LOI.

- The implementation of Private lands can be done through the consent of such landowners.

LR/ RC	Incentive Ratio					
	Area of plot in Ha					
	Upto 0.4	0.4 to 1.0	1 to 5	5 to 10	10 to 20	>20
>6	0.8	0.85	0.9	0.95	1.0	1.05
4 to 6	0.9	0.95	1.0	1.05	1.1	1.15
2 to 4	1	1.05	1.1	1.15	1.20	1.25
<2	1.1	1.15	1.2	1.25	1.30	1.35

Q11. Discuss the Maintenance deposit, Infrastructure charges & Development Charges Under Slum Rehabilitation Scheme?

Ans: The Maintenance deposit under Slum Rehabilitation Scheme is 40,000 per Rehab and Amenity Tenement.

The Infrastructure Charges under Slum Rehabilitation Scheme are 2% RR.

The Development Charges under Slum Rehabilitation Scheme is as follows-

1. Development charges for land in proportion to the free sale BUA/total BUA

2. Development charges for buildings for BUA above basic zonal FSI.

Q12. Discuss the conversion of old projects to new projects?

Ans: The Projects which were earlier approved under old regulations. If the project comes up with a change in scheme parameters, then the new regulations shall apply. If the old and new scheme is clubbed, then the relevant regulation shall apply to the relevant scheme.

Q13. Discuss Clubbing under Slum Rehabilitation Scheme?

Ans: Clubbing under Slum Rehabilitation Scheme means joint development of Slum and Non-Slum plots if the slum plot area is a minimum of 51% of the total plot area.

Q14. Where is Clubbing allowed under Slum Rehabilitation Scheme?

Ans: Clubbing is allowed between City to City, Eastern Suburbs to Eastern Suburbs, and Western Suburbs to Western Suburbs Orin adjoining wards.

Q15. Discuss Regulation 33(11) under DCPR 2034?

Ans: Regulation 33(11) of DCPR 2034 is for the construction of Permanent Transit Tenements for SRA. The tenements are handed over to Slum Rehabilitation Authority free of cost and incentive FSI is allowed for the same over and above zonal basic FSI

Location	Min Road width	Max FSI	Developers share	SRA share
City	12.0	3.00	1.9479	1.0521
City	18.0	4.00	2.3179	1.6821
Suburbs	12.0	3.00	1.75	0.75
Suburbs	18.0	4.00	2.50	1.50

Q16. What all is handed over to Tenements under Regulation 33(11) under DCPR 2034?

Ans: Tenements under Regulation 33(11) under DCPR 2034 receive Social Amenity and Society office as per the regulations. A Bike parking is also proposed under Regulation 33(10) under DCPR 2034.

Q17. Describe Special relaxations for slum schemes?

Ans: Special relaxations for slum schemes under Slum Rehabilitation Scheme are as follows:

- plot abutting min 13 m road
- No separate kitchen is necessary
- Washrooms of deficient size to be allowed.
- Joint open space for low rise building (6.00m)
- Joint open space for high rise building (12.00m)
- LOS can be reduced to 8%.
- Staircase Premium for Sale component shall be 2.5% of ASR rates
- Each tenement will be provided with scooter parking instead of Car Parking.

Q18. What is the jurisdiction of the slum rehabilitation authority?

Ans: As per 3A (1) of Chapter I-A of Maharashtra Slum Areas (Improvement, Clearance, and Redevelopment) Act, 1971 State Government of Maharashtra look Housing and Special assistance Department and through essential statuary amendments Slum Rehabilitation Authority (SRA), Mumbai was established to aid as Planning Authority for all Slum areas in the jurisdiction of Municipal Corporation of Mumbai. Later by the Government of Maharashtra Hosting Department Notification in 2014, the area of the Thane Municipal Corporation has been added to the jurisdiction of SRA

Q19. What are SRA›s Responsibilities?

Ans: SRA aims to implement the slum rehabilitation schemes by providing a single-window clearance for all the types of approvals that are essential for the project that is the formation of co-operative societies, certification of eligibility of slum dwellers, taking penal action on non-participating slum dwellers obstructing the scheme, survey, and measurement on slum land grant of permissions on buildings, leasing of rehabilitation plots, free sale plots and updating of property cards (PR cards).

The powers, duties, and functions of the Slum Rehabilitation Authority are:

1. To survey and review the existing situation about Slum areas in greater Mumbai.
2. To frame schemes for rehabilitation of slum areas.
3. To get the slum rehabilitation scheme executed.
4. To do all such other things and acts as may be needed for attaining the objective of rehabilitation of slums.

CHAPTER 19

EASE OF DOING BUSINESS AND SINGLE WINDOW CLEARANCE

The real estate sector's role is critical in any economy and is a barometer of its health. India is the second-largest direct employment creator after agriculture and has a greater multiplier effect as it affects over 250 subsidiary sectors.

However, the sector has not realized even a fraction of its potential as it has been pulled back by the in-famous opaqueness and notoriously litigious nature, one of the important reasons for not being able to attract the required institutional capital.

The Single Window Clearance Mechanism is one of the growth persuaders for the landscape. While the government has ignored this facet until now, we urge it to propose a constructive idea. Realtors must keep patience as a system like this would need several approvals and complicated infrastructure development.

Q1. What is Single Window Clearance?

Ans: The Single Window Clearance System Portal is a single-window facilitation mechanism for investors. The portal is a medium of information for investors on Government policies, incentive schemes, and the availability of infrastructure. It offers manuals to help investors to comprehend the application course for proposed investment projects. The portal will also facilitate different stakeholder departments to process applications by investors and approve them online. It also aims to build a unified repository of sector-wise investments in the State and Government policies and eventually deliver high quality and responsive service to investors.

Q2. What are the registration fees?

Ans: For Single Window System, the government of respective states as of now is Charging Rs. 500-1000 as a fee for one-time Registration. The respective Departments charge application fees as per the principal rules or acts for Application Processing.

Q3. What are the instances where Standardisation of construction norms and documentation is necessary?

Ans: Land being a state subject, all States and local bodies have separate norms on zoning policies, FSI, set back area, TDR, Slum Rehabilitation, etc. This level of difficulty and variations have led to choosing of interpretation escorting corruption leading to project delays and over expenditure. Some of the instances are.

- The difference in fire safety norms across cities.
- Occupancy certificate as a proof of completion v/s an additional requirement of completion certificate.
- Agreement to sale v/s dual agreements — one on sale for transferring an undivided share of land and a construction agreement.
- Executing property registration just at the time of possession v/s at the early stage.

For sustainable expansion, framing uniform construction norms and documentation wherever possible can benefit. We have a central policy controlling institution under the support of the National Building Code of India (NBC).

Q4. What are the major reforms taken place in an approval process?

Ans: Earlier, a building construction proposal in Mumbai required a series of approvals from about 30-35 different departments of the municipal corporation, the state government, and various central government agencies. Under the new system, developers will require 58 certifications against the earlier 119, a reduction of 52% in the number of approvals, no-objection certificates (NOCs), and BMC remarks. MCGM assumes that the new system will cut the approval time limit for a building project 60 days against the earlier 1-2 years.

Sweeping Reforms

The reforms aim to radically reduce the turnaround time for issuing construction permits and predict an overhaul of the existing permit workflow mechanism.

The salient features:

- Re-engineering of processes to save time spent on inter-departmental clearances
- Processing of 'No objection' certificates (NOCs) by MCGM's various departments even before the application for permits are submitted (pre-application processing)
- NOCs to be issued for the full potential of the plot
- Weeding out of avoidable processes. The earlier 119 approvals, NOCs, and/or remarks required for a single project have been reduced to 58 – a 52% reduction
- Use of self-certification (by developers) for approvals related to debris removal, property tax, and pest control
- Use of MCGM pre-approved external consultants for approvals related to internal layout, internal sewerage system and STP,

parking layout and manoeuvrability within the plot, stormwater drainage, mechanical and electrical works, and gardens

- Use of 'deemed' clearances wherein a delay in issuing an approval by a department beyond a pre-specified duration (ranging from 7 to 30 days) would result in automatic 'deemed' approval
- Simultaneous issuance of IOD and plinth CC within 30 days from the receipt of the proposal including site visit and approval to concessions, if any, from the competent authorities
- Commencement Certificate (further CC) to be issued within 15 days from the date of application and submission of requisite compliances
- OCC and BCC to be issued simultaneously within 15 days of application and requisite compliances
- Integration with state and central government departments has begun – approvals from the Airport Authority of India (AAI) and Ancient Monument approval from the Archaeological Survey of India (ASI) have been integrated into the new system.

Q5. What are the deadlines or maximum time limit for getting different approvals from the authorities and regulators?

Ans: According to the Federation of Indian Chambers of Commerce & Industry (FICCI) estimates, it takes long before a housing project can get formal approval from all departments concerned in the state of Maharashtra.

- Ownership certificate: 15 days
- Building layout approvals: 1 month
- A building permit from the building proposal office: 30-45 days
- Non-agricultural permission: 3 months

- NOC from tree authority: 30-60 days.
- NOC from the stormwater and drain department: 15-30 days
- NOC from sewerage department: 15-30 days
- Approval from the electric department: 15-30 days
- Approval from traffic and coordination department: 30 days
- Approval from chief fire officer: 30 days
- Environment clearance: 1 month to one year
- NOC from Archaeological Survey of India: 6 months
- NOC from pollution control board: 2 months
- Approval from Airport Authority of India: 3-4 months
- Commencement certificate: 15-30 days
- Approval from Central Ground Water Authority: 60 days
- Approval from Coastal Zone Management Authority: 6 months to 1 year
- Permission for excavation: 15-30 days
- Approvals for other common facilities: 30 days
- Permission from NHAI: 60 days.
- Permission from lift installation from PWD: 30-45 days
- Permission from Electricity Distribution Authority: 15 days
- Occupancy certificate: 60 days
- Building completion certificate from BMC: 30 days
- Permission for perpetual power and transport from BMC: 30 days
- Permission for permanent water connection: 45 days
- Permission for permanent sewerage connection: 30 days

Q6. How can real estate developers benefit from Single Window Clearance is Implemented?

Ans: A housing project would invariably miss its completion deadline even if all these departments individually delay the approvals merely by two or three days. In light of this fact, the government must introduce a single-window clearance system for housing projects without any additional delays. This has been an extended pending demand from India's real estate developers. If all sanctions can be obtained in one place without the developer having to go to various locations and yet wait for the NOCs to come by, cases of project delays would be restricted. Not only will it save a lot of time, but the human interaction that often leads to under-the-table dealings can be minimized. It then paves the way for as much transparency as possible.

The developers also view that all sanctioning authorities should intimate the applicant within the first Ten to fifteen days after the application is submitted about the progress.

Realtors and developers can focus more on sales and supply, which will indirectly help the country and its economy with increased revenue collections on the back of hiked property registrations. Fast-tracking approvals, easy documentation, decreased hassle of approvals and clearances will benefit the buyers and the realtors. With such ease in the procedure, the potential buyers also have an upper hand to cross any loans, financial barriers, and repayment. For the real estate sector to flourish with on-time execution, the approvals given by the government should be in a systemic manner. The stay in the implementation of the single window clearances is surely disturbing the timely delivery of homes.

Q7. Discuss the Objective of Ease of doing business?

Ans: The main objectives of Ease of doing business are as follows:

- Speedy Approval procedure
- Reduction in repeated number of NOC
- Obtaining parallel approvals is easier
- Time limits are defined for approvals, etc.

Q8. Discuss the Internal Services under ease of doing business?

Ans: The Internal Services under ease of doing business are as follows:

- The Developers are appointing consultants
- Consultants need to provide designs for Floor Space Index.
- A completion certificate needs to be provided by the Consultants
- The consultants have the responsibility to pass on remarks

Q9. Discuss Pro-rata Charges under the Ease of doing business?

Ans: Pro-rata charges under ease of doing business are those charges which are paid for Water and Sewer connection for full consumption of FSI. Mostly the charges are paid online.

Q10. Discuss the timeline circular under Ease of doing business?

Ans: The timeline circular under Ease of doing business is as follows:

- SUBMISSION OF PROPOSAL WITH PREREQUISITE is done within ½ a day.
- Remarks are received within 21 days.
- Getting a joint site inspection takes about 7 days.
- Obtaining an OCC cum BCC takes about 8 days.

Q11. What are the committees under Ease of doing business?

Ans: There are 5 committees under Ease of doing business. They are as follows:

- High Rise
- Heritage
- Additional FSI for stable
- Coastal Regulation Zone
- Ministry of Environment, Forest and Climate change.

CHAPTER 20

ENVIRONMENTAL LAWS

The real estate industry in India is the second prime employer after agriculture and if predicted, it is scheduled to grow at a speed of 30% over the next decade. Real Estate chiefly includes land, buildings, property and apart from them, including crops, water and minerals. The chief impact of property on the natural environment is that the property expansion process relies upon the built environment. Gradually, the concern about the environment is growing and therefore, the governments and individuals are exerting a lot of pressure on the Real Estate industry to take more account of environmental considerations.

Therefore, the legislature has formulated several laws to protect the environment from getting much destroyed and focusing on sustainable development. Let us now look into several of those laws.

Q1. What are the key laws which govern zoning or permitting and related matters regarding the use, development, and occupation of land? Briefly describe them and include environmental laws.

Ans: In India, land can be broadly categorized into the following categories

a. rural/agriculture

b. urban lands; and

c. other lands such as protected preserved forests and eco-sensitive zones.

Land that is falling under the urbanized zones is developed within the framework of town planning legislation to meet residential, commercial, institutional SEZ requirements. Information and technology (IT) parks, etc.

The Land Revenue Department governs rural/agricultural land under specific statutory enactments. It needs conversion of land from agriculture to 'non-agriculture status for development purpose as per the Master Plans or any further development permitting and definite plans.

The zoning/permits and additional related matters are region-specific and are principally governed by state laws and rules issued in this regard. For instance, all building activity must align with building bye-laws, the development code, and the national building code. Construction names are well-prescribed. The municipal laws required all buildings to obtain various certificates and permissions such as the approval for the building plans, No Objection Certificate in terms of environment, fire hazards, water assurance, sewage waste, etc. Further, certificates such as Completion Certificates and Occupation Certificates are also required to be obtained to show completion of the building in a legal manner

There are several laws governing zoning or permitting applicable to India and few States, as the case may be, and matters related to the use, development, and occupation of land in India such as:

Urban Planning and Development Laws: These are State legislation enacted to regulate zoning and land use/development regulations respective Urban Development Authorities of each State work by the provisions of the respective State/Central legislation.

Town and Country Planning Laws: Most states in India have a Department of Town besides Country Planning Act to provide for planning the development and use of rural and urban land in the respective State Wherein competent planning authorities are constituted which perform functions like formulating the Master Plan, dividing the State into zones based on their developmental potential, regulating the development in and around town, granting licenses to owners having the clear title of the land, formulating Zonal Development Plans, etc.

Master Plans: A Master Plan can be more distinctly understood as the long-term perspective plan for guiding the sustainable planned growth of the city. This document explains the planning guiding principle, policies, development code, and space requirements for several socio-economic activities supporting the population during the plan period. It is also the foundation for all infrastructure necessities. It is the subject matter of the respective State.

The Constitution of India has anticipated the absolute need to conserve and protect the environment and all its components within its framework. Article 246 of the Constitution of India rifts the subject areas of legislation between the Union and the States into 3 lists, namely:

the Union List (List I),

the State List (List II); and

the Concurrent List (List III)

which are listed under the Seventh Schedule of the Constitution of India. Matters related to environmental protection are enlisted in the Concurrent List and hence, both the State and the Union have jurisdiction for the same. Nevertheless, in matters of repugnancy, the Union will conquer.

The laws and provisions that govern with regards to environmental regulations are as follows:

1. The National Green Tribunal Act, 2010

2. The Environment Protection Act, 1986

3. The Indian Forest Act, 1972

4. The Forest Conservation Act, 1980

5. The Air (Prevention and Control of Pollution) Act, 1981

6. The Water (Prevention and Control of Pollution) Act, 1974

Concerning forest conservation, the Forest Conservation Act, 1980 regulates development limitations in forest lands and conservation of forests through State Government. The MoEF directs that an 'Environmental Impact Assessment must be organized for projects and essential certificates shall be attained from the respective State authorities functioning under the MOEF.

Q2. Can the state force landowners to sell land to it? If yes, briefly describe including price or compensation mechanism.

Ans: The State can acquire private property under eminent domain by virtue of Article 31(2) as it categorically states that the State can acquire land only for a public purpose in consideration of compensation.

The Land Acquisition Act 1894 has been the principal legislation governing the acquisition of private property by the Government. Provisions for the acquisition of land are also found in other legislation, including:

1. The Indian Forests Act 1927;

2. The Metro Railway (Construction of Works) Act 1978,

3. The National Highways Act 1956)

Q3. Which authorities control land or building use and/or environmental and occupation regulation? How do buyers get reliable information on these matters?

Ans: Local and Special Planning Authorities: A local or special planning authority is the local or special government body that is authorized by law to exercise urban planning functions for a specific area such as the Municipality of the respective urban areas, Town and Planning Commission Urban Development Authorities, etc. These authorities are formed under State Legislatures for land use planning wherein, competent planning authorities, are formed which usually go by the name of Town and Planning Department of every such State which performs functions like formulating the Master Plan, dividing the State into zones based on their developmental potential, regulating the development in and around town, granting licenses to owners having the clear title of the land, formulating Zonal Development Plans, etc., for example, DTCP Haryana, DTCP Uttar Pradesh, etc.

MOEF The apex administrative body for:

i. regulating and ensuring environmental protection;

ii. framing the environmental policy outline in the country

iii. undertaking conservation & survey of flora, fauna, forests, and wildlife; and

iv. planning, promotion, coordination, and overseeing the implementation of environmental and forestry programs

The Ministry is the nodal agency in the country for the (UNEP) United Nations Environment Programme.

Central Pollution Control Board (CPCB): Mainly executes the obligation for control and prevention of industrial pollution at the

Central Level, which is a statutory authority attached to the MoEF. The State Departments of State Pollution Control Boards and Boards are the nominated agencies to perform this function at the State level.

Environmental Information System (ENVIS): Has been established as a planned program and as a comprehensive network in environmental information collection, collation, storage, retrieval, and dissemination to varying users. ENVIS has advanced itself with a network of participating institutions or organizations.

Q4. What main permits or licenses are required for building works and/or the use of real estate?

Ans: Land Use Change Permits/Land Clearance: This is required if any land which is demarcated as ‹agricultural land› is to be converted into ‹non-agricultural land› for construction, development, and/or use of the real estate.

Zoning Permits Land in each State is differentiated and demarcated based on certain factors (like growth potential for different purposes through the Master Plans of every such State, respectively. Thus, a zoning permit may be essential for any construction activity.

The State town planner checks the city progression with the planning board and forwards the pitches to various other concerned authorities in the city as required for the issue of case-specific approvals/NOC before granting zoning approval

Building Sanctions and Approvals: The next step requires approval from the authority to sanction building plans/building permits under Building Bylaws, Master Plans, and Local Body Acts. Building approval includes the building plan and the layout approval for the construction.

1. Layout approval: The builder has to get the approval of the layout plan from implicated authorities before beginning the construction of a residential or commercial building.

   The Approved Layout Plan is as per permitted FSI (Floor Space Index) or FAR (Floor Area Ratio).

2. Building Plan: The building plan safeguards that the building complies with building laws. Once the building plan is official, the builder should begin construction work within two years and there should be no aberration from the sanctioned plan.

3. Intimation of Disapproval or similar processes or stages: Intimation of Disapproval states conditions must be complied with during different stages of an under-construction project. Intimation of Disapproval in some areas is also known as a Building Permit.

4. RERA Approval: The Real Estate Regulation and Development Act, 2016 has been passed for regulation and promotion of the real estate sector and to safeguard the sale of plot, building, or apartment as the case may be, or sale of real estate project. The Act also administers that residential and commercial projects sold by the developer or builder, during development or construction of the intended building or project, also have to get sanction under the Real Estate Regulation and Development Act, 2016 and several Rules therein, which are framed per the respective States.

Environmental Impact Assessment (EIA): The motive of an EIA is to recognize and evaluate the possible impacts (beneficial & adverse) of growth and projects on the environmental system. This exercise should be commenced early enough in the planning stage of projects to select environmentally well-suited sites, process technologies, and further environmental safeguards. Several limitations bring projects under their domain.

While all industrial projects might have some environmental effect, all of them may not be important enough to warrant intricate assessment procedures. The need for such exercises will have to be definite after a primary evaluation of the possible implications of a specific project and its location.

Environmental Clearances or Approvals: The environment advisor hired by the company prepares the Environment Impact Assessment Report which is submitted to the State level Expert Appraisal Committee which states it to the State Environment Impact Assessment Authority.

The main clearances to be obtained are:

- Fire Department Permit: A permit from any local fire department is required to be attained.

- Air and Water Pollution Control Permit: Permits for Air and Water Control are to be attained before the beginning of any real estate activity. The competent local authority of the Fire and Water department Environmental protection regulations may also require sanction be obtained before doing any construction or beginning operation.

Other permits or approvals to be obtained (if necessary) are:

1. Coastal Regulatory Zone (CRZ) clearance is obtained wherever required by the Coastal Zone Management Authority.

2. Ancient Monument Approval by the Archaeological Survey of India.

3. NOC from Airport Authority of India by Civil Aviation Department/Airport Authority of India.

4. NOC from the Sewerage Department (Municipal).

5. NOC from the Drain Department and Storm Water (Municipal).

6. NOC from the Electric Department (Municipal), etc.

Q5. Are they any regulations on the safeguarding of historic monuments in your jurisdiction? If yes, when and how are they expected to affect the transfer of rights in real estate or development change of use?

Ans: As per the Ancient Monuments and Archaeological Sites and Remains, 1958, an ‹Ancient Monument is defined under "Section 2(a) of the act as any structure, erection or monument, or any tumulus or place of interment, or any cave, rock sculpture. inscription or monolith, which is of historical archaeological or artistic interest and which has been in existence for not less than 100 years, and includes:

1. the remains of an ancient monument,

2. the site of an ancient monument.

3. such portion of land adjoining the site of an ancient monument as may be required for fencing or covering in or otherwise preserving such monument; and

4. the means of access to, and convenient inspection of an ancient monument."

If the Central Government detains that the protected monument is at risk of being destroyed, misused, injured, or allowed to fall into decay, it may undertake the maintenance of the protected monument.

Q6. Briefly outline any regulatory necessities for the assessment and administration of the energy performance of buildings in the jurisdiction.

Ans: As per Section 2(f) of the Energy Conservation Act, 2001: "Energy conservation building codes means the norms and standards of energy consumption expressed in terms of per sq. m of the area where energy is used and comprises the location of the building."

To restraint energy consumption in buildings, the Indian Government issued the (ECBC) Energy Conservation Building Code in 2007. However, the impact of the ECBC depends on the efficiency of its enforcement and compliance. Now, the mainstream buildings in India are not ECBC compliant. Whether the projected targets can be accomplished depends on how the code enforcement system is planned and implemented.

Even though the progress of ECBC lies in the hands of the national Government the Bureau of Energy Efficiency under the Ministry of Power, the adoption and implementation of ECBC mostly depends on State and local governments

Q7. Briefly explain the nature and scope of any regulatory measures for reducing carbon dioxide emissions including any mandatory emissions trading scheme.

Ans: India has introduced a multi-faceted policy framework that seeks to address climate change control by reducing greenhouse gas emissions.

In June 2008, the Indian Government launched India's first National Action Plan on Climate Change with eight-core 'national missions' focused on the broader themes of mitigation, adaptation, and stakeholder engagement.

The National Action Plan is stated in India's Five-Year Plan which guides comprehensive economic policy. Climate change goals are included in this plan: reduce emissions intensity in line with India's Copenhagen pledge and add 300,000 MW of renewable energy capacity.

The current Government has taken steps to scale up clean energy production and has initiated a shift in India's deportment in international climate negotiations. The Government's acknowledgement of the threat posed by climate change is reflected in one of the Government's first initiatives: rename the environment ministry from the Union Ministry of Environment and Forests to the Ministry of Environment Forest and Climate Change.

Q8. Are there any other regulatory measures (not already mentioned, which aim to improve the sustainability of both newly constructed and existing buildings?

Ans: There exist regulatory measures which aim to improve the sustainability of newly constructed and existing buildings as mentioned below:

Model Building Bye-Laws 2016: The Town and Country Planning Organisation, Ministry of Urban Development has made an effort to prepare 'Model Building Bye-Laws 2016' to guide the State Governments, Urban Local Bodies, Urban Development Authorities, and others. The salient features of the act provide for provisions for Safety and Security, Adoption for Modern Construction Technology Barrier-Free Environment Environmental Concerns, Swachh Bharat Mission, Rain Water Harvesting, and Effects of Communication Technology Ease of Doing Business.

Powers of entry and inspection: The Environment Protection Act, 1986, under the ambit of Section 10, permits any person authorized by the Central Government to have a right to enter, at all rational times with such aid as he considers necessary, any place:

a. To perform any of the functions of the Central Government entrusted to him,

b. To determine whether and, if so, in what manner, any such functions are to be performed; or

c. To examine and test any equipment, industrial plant, record, etc. or for searching any building and for seizing any such equipment, industrial plant, record, register, document or other material objects if he has reason to believe that it may furnish evidence of the commission of an offence punishable under this Act or the rules made thereunder or that such seizure is necessary to prevent or mitigate environmental pollution.

Air (Prevention and Control) of Pollution Act, 1981: It aims at curbing environmental pollution by targeting sources that cause par-standard air pollution through harmful oxides, particulate matter, and sulfides. It provides provisions for State and Central Boards to declare the area as a pollution control area.

Ministry of Environment and Forests Government of India (Office Memorandum): The Ministry had issued rules for high-rise buildings,

Q9. What is the acceptable noise level at the construction site and what could be the possible precautions taken?

Ans: Noise from construction and civil engineering works. – Noise from construction sites is usually far worse than noise originating from industries. There are two main reasons for this. One is that wherever construction takes place like the erection of roads, bridges and buildings noise emissions levels are higher. The other is that civil engineering tools are inherently noisy. The worst of these pieces of tools, from the noise generation point of view, are the following:

Equipment	Noise levels t15m.
Tractor-scraper	93 dB
Rock drill	87 dB
Unmuffled concrete breaker	85 dB
Hand-held tree saw	82 dB
Large rotary diesel compressor	80 dB
11/2 tonne dumper truck Diesel	75 dB
Concrete mixer	75 dB

In the era of fast development of buildings and roads, the demolition & repair activities, along with the massive machines used for the purposes create a great deal of noise to the annoyance of the public living near construction sites. Hence such works are also a potential source of noise pollution.

Precautions in Construction Activities. –

1. Acoustic barriers should be placed near construction sites.

2. The maximum noise levels near the construction site should be limited to 75 dB (A) Leg (5 min) in industrial areas and 65 dB (A) Leg (5 min) in other areas.

3. There should be fencing around the construction site to prevent people from coming near the site.

4. Materials need to be stockpiled and unused equipment to be placed between noisy operating equipment and other areas.

5. Constructing temporary earth and around the site using soil etc., which normally is hauled away from the construction site.

Q10. Discuss Public Sanitary Convenience under Environmental Sustainability?

Ans: Public Sanitary Convenience under Environmental Sustainability is discussed under Part 12 of DCPR 2034. PSC blocks may be constructed on Municipal Plots and should be available for public usage after taking approvals from the Commissioner.

Q11. Describe the location of Public Sanitary Convenience Blocks under Environmental Sustainability?

Ans: The location of Public Sanitary Convenience Blocks under Environmental Sustainability will be such that it is easily available for public usage.

Q12. Who will maintain the Public Sanitary Convenience Blocks under Environmental Sustainability?

Ans: The maintenance of the Public Sanitary Convenience Blocks under Environmental Sustainability will be done by the User of such plots where the PSC block is situated or done by any person the Commissioner will decide.

Q13. Describe the Public Sanitary Convenience Blocks under Environmental Sustainability which has an area of more than 4000 Sq. Mt?

Ans: The Public Sanitary Convenience Blocks under Environmental Sustainability has an area of more than 4000 Sq. Mt shall have at least 2 Urinals & toilets each for the Gents and Ladies and it should also have one toilet for the differently-abled persons and one urinal for children.

Q14. Describe the Public Sanitary Convenience Blocks under Environmental Sustainability which has an area of more than 2000 Sq. Mt?

Ans: The Public Sanitary Convenience Blocks under Environmental Sustainability has an area of more than 2000 Sq. Mt shall have atleast 1 toilet and 2 urinals for ladies and gents and one toilet for differently-abled persons and one urinal for children.

Q15. Describe the permissible FSI for Public Sanitary Convenience Blocks under Environmental Sustainability?

Ans: The Public Sanitary Convenience Blocks under Environmental Sustainability is free of Floor Space Index.

Q16. Discuss Rain Water Harvesting?

Ans: The Rain Water Harvesting is provided in case of Development of plots having an area of more than 500 sq. m.

Q17. Discuss the systems that must be adopted for harvesting the rainwater?

Ans: The following systems may be adopted for harvesting the rainwater:

- Open well of a minimum diameter of 1 m and a minimum depth of 6 m.
- The recharge of groundwater may be done through a bore well around which a pit of one-meter width may be excavated up to a depth of at least 3 m.
- After storage, the surplus rainwater may be recharged into the ground through percolation pits or trenches or a combination of pits and trenches.

- Perforated concrete slabs shall be provided on the pits/trenches, etc.

Q18. Discuss how the terrace is connected to the Open Well?

Ans: The terrace is connected to the Open Well through PVC pipes and filter media. There shall be at least two rainwater pipes of 100 mm dia for the efficient discharge of rainwater for a rooftop area of 100sq. m.

Q19. Discuss where Rain Water Harvesting structures to be sited?

Ans: The Rain Water Harvesting structures shall be sited as not to endanger the building's stability.

Q20. Discuss the Installation of Solar Water Heating under Environmental Sustainability?

Ans: the Installation of Solar Water Heating under Environmental Sustainability is mandatory for Hospitals, Hotels, Guest Houses, Police/Army Barracks, Canteens, Laboratories and Research Institutions, Hostels of Schools and Colleges, and other Institutions.

Q21. Why Solar water heating is mandatory in Hospitals?

Ans: The Solar water heating systems shall be mandatory in hospitals and hotels, as the hot water requirement is continuous. In such buildings, the system shall be provided with auxiliary electrical backup.

Q22. Discuss the pre-requisites for Installation of Solar Water Heating under Environmental Sustainability?

Ans: The pre-requisites for Installation of Solar Water Heating under Environmental Sustainability are as follows:

- Buildings where Solar Water Heating systems are installed, will have an open sunny roof area available to install the system.
- The roof loading adopted in the design of such a building should be at least 50 kg/sq. m
- Solar Water Heating systems can also be integrated with the building design.
- New buildings of aforesaid types to be constructed shall have an installed hot water line from the rooftop and also insulated distribution pipelines
- The capacity of the SWH system to be installed on the building shall be decided based on the average occupancy of the building.

Q23. Describe the Waste Water Recycling and Reuse?

Ans: The Waste Water Recycling and Reuse main focus is not on treatment but reuse. The provisions issued by the Government of India from time to time shall have the provision for recycling and reuse of wastewater.

Q24. Discuss what shall be included in Waste Water Recycling and Reuse?

Ans: The following must be included in Waste Water Recycling and Reuse:

- Wastewater other than from water closets, laundries, and hospitals shall be recycled.
- The system shall not constitute a nuisance of foul gases.

- The wastewater recycling system shall be designed considering the anticipated occupancy load and seasonal fluctuations in discharge.
- Separating of Waste Water

Q25. Discuss the Reuse of Waste Water?

Ans: The Reuse of Waste Water must be done in the following manner:

- The treated wastewater shall be used only for gardening, toilet flushing, landscape, irrigation, cooling towers, car washing etc.
- The output water quality shall be as per the standards of non-potable water as may be prescribed by the MPCB.
- The owner must include a clause that a recycled wastewater system has been provided in the development.

Q26. Give a brief on Sewage Treatment Plant and Disposal?

Ans: The Sewage Treatment Plant and Disposal›s main focus is treating and reducing BOD within permissible limits. The provisions issued by the Government of India from time to time shall have the provision for Sewage Treatment Plant and Disposal.

Q27. What all shall the Sewage Treatment Plant and Disposal should Comply?

Ans: the Sewage Treatment Plant and Disposal should comply with the following:

1. The Sewage Treatment Plant structure shall be of a compact design.
2. No foul odour to be present near the Sewage Treatment Plant area.

3. Sewage Treatment Plant will not require continuous monitoring.

4. The water treated in such plants should be safe for disposal.

5. The water after the treatment should be of nonportable standards.

6. A clause must be included by the owner that Sewage Treatment Plant provided for the development is as per the standards of the Pollution Control Board.

Q28. Discuss Solid Waste Segregation in brief?

Ans: The Apartments do solid Waste Segregation as per the guidelines of the competent authority of that area. The Apartment provides separate bins to collect Dry waste, Wet waste, and hazardous waste. A separate dedicated area is there for waste collection before they are sent for disposal.

Q29. How much waste does a common household Contain?

Ans: A common household contains merely 50% of Organic waste and 50% of Inorganic Waste.

Q30. Does the Purchase Agreement contain any such clause for Wet waste Treatment?

Ans: Yes, the Purchase Agreement contains a clause for Wet waste Treatment. It also says that the treatment will be done as per the guidelines of the competent Authority.

Q31. Discuss Tree plantation provisions for conserving/ preserving Bio-Diversity?

Ans: The Development should be in such a manner that one should take utmost care to protect the existing trees on the land which is going to be developed.

If it is required that the trees need to be cut then for each tree cut, then twice the number of trees needs to be planted. It should be taken into the picture that only local trees are planted and not fancy trees.

It should be taken into the picture that every plot must have at least-regu

a. At the rate of five indigenous trees per 100 sq. m or part thereof of the said recreational space, to be grown within the entire plot.

b. At the rate of one indigenous tree per 80 sq. m or part of it to be grown in a plot for which a sub-division or layout is not needed.

Q32. What are the main environmental laws related to real estate?

Ans: The main environmental legislation relating to real estate development is as follows:

- Wildlife Protection Act, 1972 (Wildlife Act)
- Water Prevention and Control of Pollution Act, 1974.
- Environment (Protection) Act, 1986
- Air Prevention and Control of Pollution Act, 1981
- Forest Conservation Act, 1980 Forest Act
- Hazardous Waste Management and Handling Rules, 1989
- Coastal Regulation Zone Notification, 2011

Q34. What are the regulatory authorities concerning real estate in India?

Ans: The following are the regulatory authorities related to real estate development in India:

a. National Green Tribunal (NGT)

b. The Ministry of Environment & Forests (MOEF)

c. Central and State Pollution Control Board

d. Coastal Regulation Zone Management Authority

e. National Board of Wild Life (NBWF)

f. Forest Settlement Officer

Q35. What is MOEF?

Ans: MOEF means the ministry of environment and forests which is the apex administrative body responsible for the regulation, planning, promotion, and coordination of forest and environmental plans in our country.

Q36. What is freehold estate?

Ans: A freehold estate is an interest in land that has an indefinite duration. The freehold can be absolute ownership called the fee simple absolute or an interest in the land for the possessor's life, in either case, it is absurd to say exactly how long the estate will last.

- If one owns the property outright, his/her estate will last until he/she sells or transfers it.
- It will last until the owner's demise or another stated individual in the case of a life estate.

Q37. What is a lease-hold estate?

Ans: A leasehold estate is one whose termination date is typically known. A one-year lease, for example, will expire indeed at the time stated in the lease agreement.

www.ingramcontent.com/pod-product-compliance
Lightning Source LLC
Chambersburg PA
CBHW020729180526
45163CB00001B/166